Contents

chapter 1

cute pets and furry friends 14

chapter 2

into the wild 70

introduction

Loopy animals are the coolest critters around! This book includes 25 fun animal characters to make using rubber bands, with plenty of further suggestions for making your own designs. Each one has a skill level of one star (easy), two stars (medium), or three stars (advanced). Once you have made your creatures, turn them into bag danglers, keyrings, magnets, brooches, and more!

Begin with the techniques section so that you can find out what materials you need and brush up on your basic skills, ready to work your way through the projects. The first chapter, "Cute Pets and Furry Friends," shows you how to create dogs, cats, and bunnies and to personalize them so they look like your own pets, as well as ponies, sheep, and pigs so you can make your own loopy farm.

Chapter 2, "Into the Wild," has instructions for more exotic animals. Here you can learn how to loop dolphins, octopuses, and penguins for an underwater lagoon, invent a woodland wonderland with foxes and deer, and create a safari scene with elephants, monkeys, and brightly colored tropical parrots! And there are also wild critters that you might see closer to home in your back yard, such as dragonflies and bees.

Loopy animals are an ideal summer camp or sleepover activity. It's such fun for you and your friends to help each other master a new design and experiment with colors to make your critters look different from each other. The animals make wonderful gifts if made into brooches or keyrings. Why not make a stash, set up a stall at your school fair, and sell your wares to raise money for your school or a charity organization?

So go and get your loom, bands, and hooks ready to make some fabulous new animal designs!

Loopy Loom

Rubber Band

ANIMALS

25 fun designs
for jewelry and
accessories

Lucy Hopping

CICO BOOKS

LONDON NEW YORK

Published in 2015 by CICO Kidz
An imprint of Ryland Peters & Small
341 E 116th St, New York NY 10029
20–21 Jockey's Fields, London WC1R 4BW
www.rylandpeters.com

10 9 8 7 6 5 4 3 2 1

A CIP catalog record for this book is
available from the Library of Congress
and the British Library.

ISBN: 978-1-78249-183-5

Printed in China

Editor: Sarah Hoggett
Designer: Alison Fenton
Illustrator: Louise Turpin
Photographer: Emma Mitchell
Stylist: Rob Merrett

In-house editor: Carmel Edmonds
In-house designer: Fahema Khanam
Art director: Sally Powell
Production controller: Sarah Kulasek-Boyd
Publishing manager: Penny Craig
Publisher: Cindy Richards

Lucy Hopping works as an Art and Craft Product
Developer in the toy industry, designing and developing
kits to teach children various crafts. This has taken her to
UK and international trade fairs and to showrooms and
factories in the Far East. In her spare time, Lucy enjoys
making stitched, crocheted, and knitted products to sell
at local craft fairs and on craft websites. She is passionate
about inspiring young people to get crafting, as well as
making items in her own right. She is the author of
Rubber Band Bracelets, *Friendship Bracelets*, co-author of
Handmade Glamping, and a contributor to *Crafting for
Girls*, all published by CICO Books.

tools

It doesn't take much to create your loopy animals—a loom, a variety of colored bands, and a few crochet hooks. In this section we guide you through all the tools you need and how to use them.

Looms

The animal projects in this book are all made using a loom. At the beginning of each project, we have told you what size loom you need, whether the pegs should be set up in a square or diagonal format, and what direction the arrows on your loom should be facing.

Plastic loom

The most popular type of loom is made from plastic and can be bought from craft stores or online. Most looms are made from three strips of 13 pegs that can be pulled apart and attached together in a square or diagonal layout. You can also buy extra looms and join them together to make wider and longer looms, which is very handy for some of the larger projects.

Top view of peg   **Side view of peg**

Each peg is hollow, so you can insert your hook into it, and has an open back, which makes it easy to catch the band in the tip of your hook to loop it over.

Other equipment

As well as your loom, you will also need a few good strong crochet hooks and rubber bands. Once you have completed your project, you may want to turn it into something—in which case you will need split rings, ring blanks, hairclips, and so on.

Hooks

The looms that you buy from craft stores or online generally come with a plastic hook, but if you break your hook, use a US size G/6 (4mm) metal crochet hook instead. It will be much stronger and won't bend when you are working on projects that have a lot of tension in them.

For the projects in this book, you will often need a few spare hooks as holding hooks. These are used when making separate limbs, eyes, and other body pieces that are attached to the main body later on.

The holding hook can hold more than one item at a time, and you may find it easier to use a knitting needle or pencil if you don't have lots of crochet hooks to hand.

You can still make use of the hook that comes with ready-made plastic looms. The thicker end of the plastic hook can help you prise apart the strips of the loom when you need to assemble them in a different format or join two or more looms together (see above).

Clip-on earring **Brooch pin** **Ring blank**

Rubber bands

This is where you can let your imagination run wild! There are many different types of band available, including colored, jelly, neon, glitter, metallic, glow-in-the-dark, and even scented bands!

Some bands are better quality and stronger than others, so always try and buy good-quality ones; you will find the cheaper ones tend to snap during the looping and pulling off the loom stages, which is very frustrating!

Try organizing your bands into colors and separating them into a plastic segmented storage box or individual sandwich bags. This makes things much easier, as there is nothing more annoying than searching for that last elusive pink band to complete your project and not having one!

Jewelry findings

To turn your animal charms into accessories such as clip-on earrings, rings, and key rings, you will need a good supply of metal jewelry findings. Available in craft stores, online, and in beading stores, these are a really effective way of showing off your creations!

To make hair accessories, try visiting your local supermarket or accessories store for plain hairbands, elastics, and hairclips. There is a wide range of colors, sizes, and shapes available, so you can match them with the rubber bands you have used for that particular project!

Glue

To attach the jewelry findings to your animal charms, you will need a glue gun or some Superglue. These are both very strong and dangerous glues to use, so ask an adult to supervise you at all times.

A glue gun is a special tool that is plugged in and heats up. When the gun is warm enough, the glue stick in the gun melts and can be squeezed out using the trigger. The glue is very hot when it comes out, so be very careful not to burn yourself. It cools down and hardens very quickly, though, so it is a very speedy way of completing your projects.

Superglue is a clear and very strong chemical glue. It can be bought from craft stores, hardware stores, and online. Do not touch the glue, as it is very sticky and will stick itself to everything. Make sure you read the instructions carefully before you use it.

Felt

Once you have glued your jewelry finding to your charm, the back can look very messy. Small pieces of felt stuck over the back hide all the glue and also add strength to the piece (see page 12). Craft felt comes in a wide variety of colors, so you can be sure of finding one that suits your project—and all you need are tiny scraps, so be sure to save leftover felt from other craft projects.

Clips

Plastic clips are used to secure the last loops in a project together so that it does not fall apart. They come in three main designs—C-clips, S-clips, and locking clips.

They are usually in bright colors so you can match them to the design of the bracelet or necklace. The only projects that use clips in this book are the Bunny and Carrot Bracelet (page 56) and during the making of Ollie the Octopus (page 124). However, you may wish to make some of your other animals

S-clip   **C-clip**   **Locking C-clip**

into charms and attach them as we have with the bunny bracelet, so it is worth having a stash anyway. Most packs of bands come with some clips, so you will not need to buy them specially.

techniques

There are a few simple techniques to master before you try out the projects in this book, such as laying out your bands, hooking them, and finishing off the designs. Read these tips carefully before you start any of the projects to ensure that they are a success and do not fall apart when you pull them off the loom!

Laying out your bands

The first step in making your animal is to lay out your bands.

At the beginning of each project, there is a diagram to show what type of loom set-up you need. Check whether it is a square or diagonal format and adjust your loom accordingly.

Usually the bands are laid with the arrows on the loom pointing toward you and the open side of the pegs facing you.

Lay your bands in the order given in the instructions. If you do not lay them in the correct order, when you come to hook the bands and pull the project off the loom it may fall apart or look different from the picture.

Always push the bands down on the pegs, especially if there are lots of bands on the pegs. This makes it easier to hook them and also prevents them from falling off the pegs.

In the projects in this book, you don't always lay just one band over a hook: sometimes you have to twist single bands into a figure-eight shape (we call this a doubled-over single), and sometimes you have to lay out pairs of bands. The project instructions will tell you what you need to do, so always read them very carefully when laying out your bands.

Single band

Pair of bands

Doubled-over single band

Cap bands

A cap band is added to the top of a peg once all the bands have been laid out. This is a band that is twisted around the peg—four times usually—and forms a stopper for the project, so that the animal does not fall apart when

you pull it from the loom. These bands are not hooked; instead, you pick up the band below the cap band and hook that band over its opposing peg. Cap bands are normally placed on the last peg of a section.

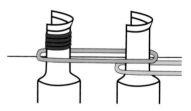

Holding bands

Holding bands are laid out after the main bands, before the project is hooked. They hold the project together and make it a solid item rather than a series of long strips. The clearest way to demonstrate this is in Ollie the Octopus (page 124). Note that the bands that have holding bands across them become a solid piece of body, whereas the legs (which do not have holding bands) hang loose.

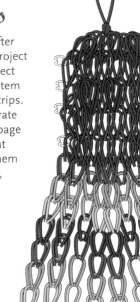

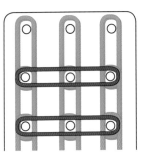

Holding bands are laid either straight if the loom format is square (as in Ollie the Octopus) or in a triangular formation if the loom is set up in a diagonal format (as in Lola the Cat, page 34). When hooked, the effect is the same.

To shape your animal you can increase or decrease the number of holding bands. For a tight effect, use doubled-over single bands; for a fairly loose finish, use single bands; for a chunky animal, use pairs of bands. You can even wrap the holding bands around the pegs one and a half times to give your animal a curved body, as in Dolly the Dolphin on page 120.

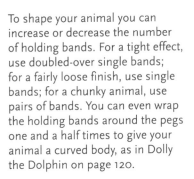

Hooking your bands

Once you have laid out all your bands, make sure that the arrows on the loom are facing toward you. This means that the open side of the peg is facing you, which makes it easier to get the hook into the peg and to pick up the band with the tip of your hook.

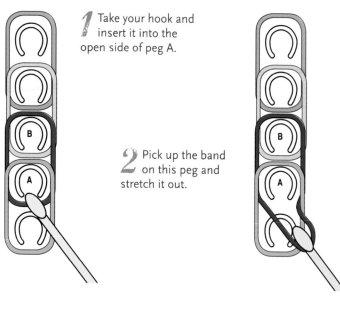

1 Take your hook and insert it into the open side of peg A.

2 Pick up the band on this peg and stretch it out.

3 Now hook the band that you've just picked up onto the peg that the other end of the band is on. This peg may be above, to the side of, or diagonally opposite the first peg. I call this "hooking it over the opposing peg."

Opposing peg (B) is above the first peg (A)

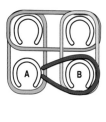

Opposing peg (B) is to the side of the first peg (A)

Opposing peg (B) is diagonally above the first peg (A)

4 A teardrop shape is formed, which traps the ends of the previous band so that your project doesn't unravel. Repeat the hooking process in the order shown in your project.

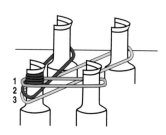

Note: If there are lots of layers of bands in your project, you will work from the top band downward. So you would hook the blue band first, then the red band, and finally the green band.

Making eyes

In most of the projects in this book, the eyes are made using the following technique.

1 Wrap a band around your hook four times. The color you choose will be the color of the eye, so black or blue generally work best.

2 Twist a single white band into a figure-eight shape and pull one end of it through the four loops on your hook. Hook the other end of the white band over your hook.

3 Repeat steps 1 and 2 with another black (or blue) and another white band, then pull a single band through all the loops on your hook. Hook the other end of the single band over your hook. Leave on a holding hook.

Attaching a separate head

In some of the projects (for example, the pig on page 48, the sheep on page 66, and the deer on page 106), the head piece is made separately and then attached to the body later on. There are two ways of doing this; both work in a similar way, and it's up to you which you prefer using.

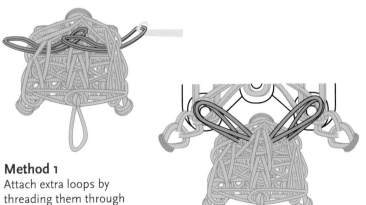

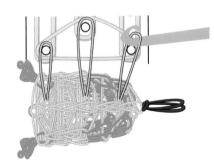

Method 1
Attach extra loops by threading them through the back of the head, as with the pig on page 48.

Method 2
Insert your hook into the back of the head and use some of the loops already in the head.

Pulling your project off the loom

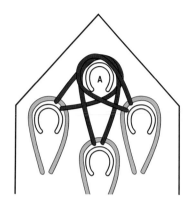

Just one peg on the top row

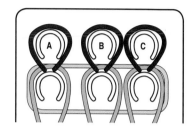

Three pegs on the top row

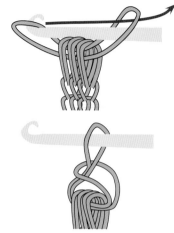

Completing a project

Once all your bands are hooked over, and before you pull them off the loom, double-check that you have teardrop shapes between each peg. These teardrops keep all the bands together and stop the project from falling apart when you pull it off the loom.

If you do notice a mistake, you can unhook your bands, working backward in order in the way you hooked them, and fix the mistake before it's too late and you end up with a loopy mess!

Once you are satisfied, insert your hook into the top row of pegs in that design. You may have just one peg or more to insert your hook into. Pick up all the loops on those pegs and gently pull the project off the loom. Do not pull too hard or too quickly or the bands may snap.

You should now have a project on your hook!

To complete, thread a single band through all the loops on your hook, then thread one end of the band through the other, and pull tight to secure. This will hold all the bands together and ensure they don't fall apart. To neaten, you can pull the loose band through the back of the piece with your hook to hide it.

Making your animals into accessories

Once you have completed your animals, it's time to decide what to do with them! Make keyrings and charms with them by attaching split rings, attach them to simple bracelets or necklaces as we did with the Bunny and Carrot Bracelet on page 56, or glue them to hairbands, clips, rings, and more to make funky accessories.

When you attach your animal to a jewelry finding, add a small patch of felt on top before the glue dries—this will hide the glue and make a neater finish.

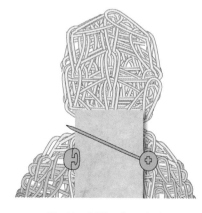

Attaching felt to a brooch pin

tips and tricks

• PRACTICE MAKES PERFECT! DON'T BE DISCOURAGED IF YOUR FIRST ATTEMPT AT A DESIGN DOESN'T WORK OUT—JUST PULL THE BANDS OFF AND START AGAIN!

• ALWAYS GET OUT YOUR BANDS BEFORE YOU START A PROJECT. AS WELL AS MAKING THE LAYING-OUT STAGE QUICKER, THIS ALSO MEANS YOU CAN MAKE SURE YOU HAVE ENOUGH OF EACH COLOR TO COMPLETE THE PROJECT.

• WHEN LAYING OUT THE BANDS, ALWAYS MAKE SURE THAT YOU HAVE YOUR LOOM FACING THE CORRECT WAY, AS SPECIFIED IN THE INSTRUCTIONS. USUALLY THIS IS WITH THE ARROWS ON THE LOOM FACING TOWARD YOU, BUT SOME ARE WORKED THE OTHER WAY ROUND.

• ALWAYS LAY OUT THE BANDS IN THE ORDER GIVEN IN THE INSTRUCTIONS. A LITTLE MISTAKE CAN RESULT IN AN ANIMAL THAT DOESN'T HOLD TOGETHER OR LOOKS DIFFERENT FROM WHAT YOU WERE EXPECTING.

• PRESS THE BANDS DOWN ON THE LOOM AS FAR AS POSSIBLE, ESPECIALLY WHEN THERE ARE LOTS OF BANDS ON EACH PEG. THIS WILL PREVENT THEM FROM FALLING OFF THE LOOM WHEN YOU ARE HOOKING.

• WHEN HOOKING THE BANDS, ALWAYS HAVE THE ARROWS POINTING TOWARD YOU AND, IF YOU ARE USING A PLASTIC LOOM, THE OPEN SIDE OF THE PEGS FACING YOU.

• ALWAYS PICK UP THE TOP BAND ON THE PEG (EXCLUDING THE CAP BAND) AND WORK DOWNWARD WHEN LOOPING YOUR BANDS.

• BEFORE PULLING YOUR PROJECT OFF THE LOOM, CHECK THAT ALL THE BANDS HAVE BEEN HOOKED AS REQUIRED. THE HOOKING CREATES A TEARDROP SHAPE, AND EVERY BAND SHOULD BE TRAPPED IN ONE OF THESE TEARDROP SHAPES.

chapter 1

cute pets and
furry friends

A must-loop for all dog lovers! These pastel-colored poodles are great fun to make and even better to give to friends and family.

loopy poodle

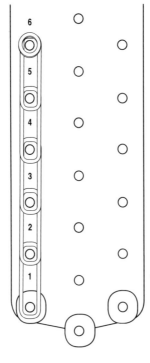

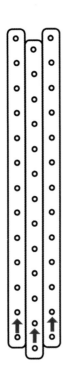

LOOM SETUP

Set up your loom in the diagonal format—3 pegs wide x 13 pegs long (see page 6).

1 First, make the poodle's legs. With the arrows on the loom pointing away from you, lay five doubled-over single white bands on the loom in the order shown. Twist a white band four times around the last peg to make a cap band.

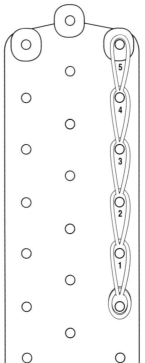

2 Turn the loom around so that the arrows are pointing toward you. Insert your hook into the peg with the cap band, pick up the bottom white band, and hook it over its opposing peg. Repeat all the way up the loom.

3 Insert your holding hook into the top peg, gently pull the leg off the loom, and place it to one side, leaving it on the hook. Repeat steps 1–3 to make another leg.

4 With the arrows on the loom pointing toward you, place two bands between each pair of pegs in the colors and order shown. Twist a white band four times around each of the two bottom pegs to make cap bands.

5 Twist a black band four times around a hook, then thread another doubled-over single black band through the center, using a third hook.

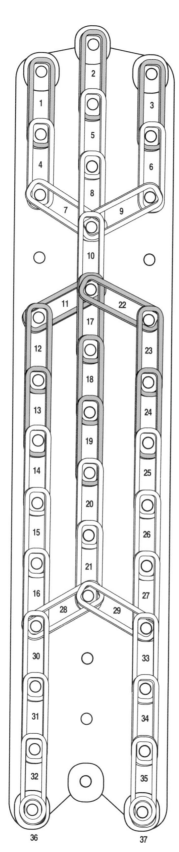

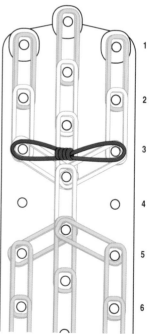

6 Place this over the pegs on row 3, as shown.

loopy poodle **17**

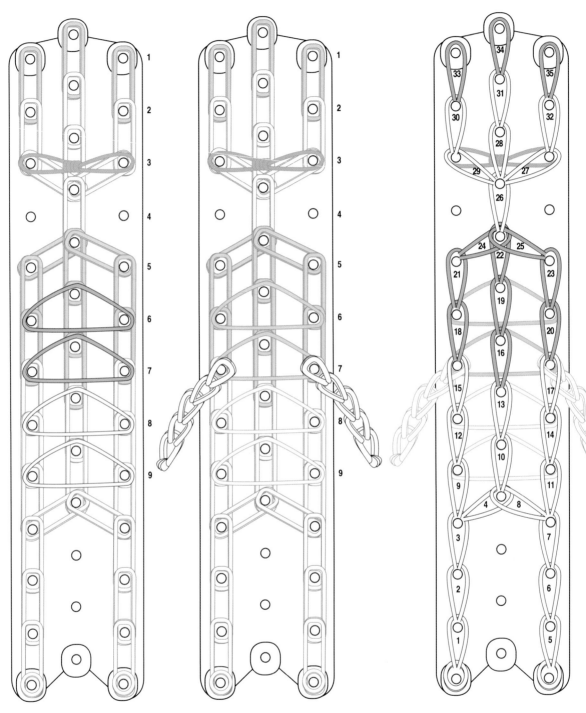

7 Place single turquoise bands in a triangle shape over rows 6 and 7 and doubled-over single white bands over rows 8 and 9.

Place the legs you made in steps 1–3 over the outer pegs on row 7.

Insert your hook into the bottom right peg and then hook the bands over their opposing pegs in the order shown.

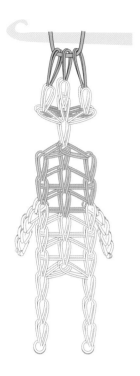

10 Insert your hook into the loops on the top three pegs and gently pull the poodle off the loom, leaving it on the hook. Insert a turquoise band through the loops on the hook, then thread one end of the loop through the other and pull tight to secure. Pull at the legs to shape them into a sitting poodle shape.

To make the poodle into a keyring, thread the top loop onto a split ring.

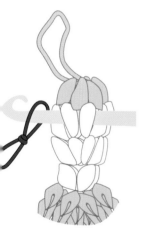

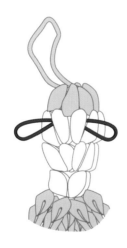

11 Tie a knot in the center of a black band. Insert your hook into the center loops at the back of the poodle's head, then pull the black band through these loops.

12 Turn the head around and pull the loop ends through to the front of the face to make eyes.

13 To make the ears and tail, twist a turquoise band around a hook four times, pull a single white band through, thread one end of the white band through the other, and pull tight to secure. Make two more in the same way.

14 Insert your hook into the area you want to attach the ears and tail to pull the long end through, and loop it over the turquoise bobble. Pull tight to secure.

15 Add the collar by placing two pink bands over the poodle's head. Finally, make the colored ankles by wrapping a turquoise band three times around each leg.

tessa the turtle

This cute little turtle is one of my favorite rubber-band animals! She makes a great pencil topper, and the shell design gives you a chance to experiment with cool color combinations.

SKILL LEVEL ★ ★ ★

You Will Need

2 looms

52 jade bands

29 white bands

2 dark turquoise bands

11 orange bands

24 purple bands

14 pink bands

Hook

Holding hooks

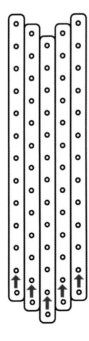

LOOM SETUP

Set up your loom in the V format—5 pegs wide x 13 pegs long (see page 6). You will need to join two looms together widthwise.

1 First make the legs. Take two jade bands and twist them three times around your hook. Pull two single jade bands through the loops on your hook.

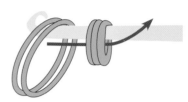

2 Repeat with another two single jade bands, leaving the loops on the hook.

3 Repeat steps 1 and 2 to make three more legs. Put to one side.

4 Now make the eyes. Twist two white bands twice around your hook, then twist a dark turquoise band around the hook six times, then twist the first white bands around your hook two more times.

5 Pull two single jade bands through all the loops on your hook.

6 With the eye made in steps 4 and 5 still on your hook, wrap another single jade band around the hook three times and pull those loops onto the end of the eye. Put to one side.

7 Repeat steps 4 through 6 to make a second eye.

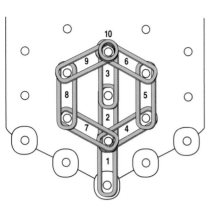

To make your turtle into a pencil topper, insert a pencil up its bottom into the shell cavity!

To make the head, lay out pairs of jade bands in the order shown, with the arrows on the loom pointing away from you. Add a single jade cap band to the top peg, twisting it around the peg three times.

Place a doubled-over single jade band in a triangular shape over the pegs on row 1 and the center peg. Then repeat with another doubled-over single jade band across the pegs on row 2 and the center peg.

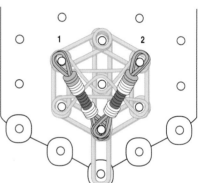

10 Place the eyes you made earlier diagonally on the loom as shown.

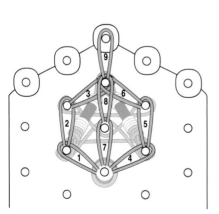

11 Turn the loom around. Insert your hook into the bottom peg, under the cap band, and hook the bands in the order shown.

12 Insert your hook into the top peg, through all four bands, and gently pull the head off the loom, leaving it on the hook. Put to one side.

13 Now make the shell of the turtle. With the arrows on the loom pointing away from you, lay out single white bands in the order shown. Then lay the loops of the legs (made in steps 1–3) onto the shoulders and hips of the turtle, as shown.

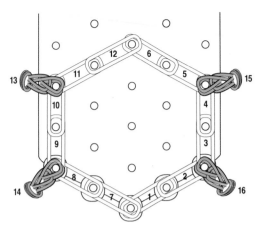

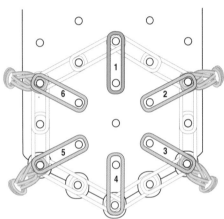

14 Lay a single jade band as band 1 (this will become the tail), and then single orange bands in the order shown.

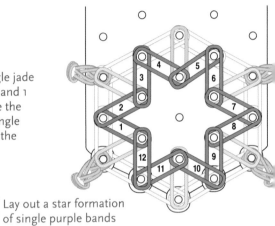

15 Lay out a star formation of single purple bands in the order shown.

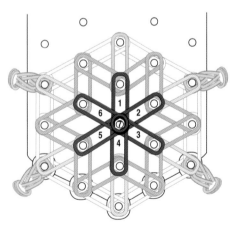

16 Complete the underside of the shell by laying a star of single pink bands in the order shown. Add a pink cap band to the center peg, twisting it around the peg four times.

17 Turn the loom around so that the arrows on the loom are pointing toward you, and start hooking bands from the center cap band outward in the order shown. Place the head you made earlier over the top peg.

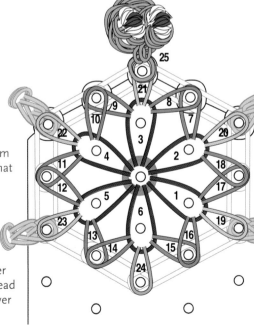

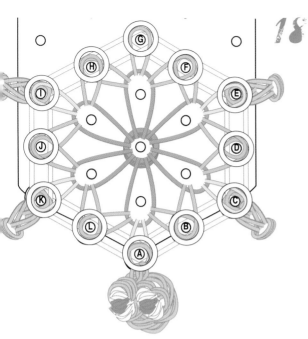

18 Lay single white bands over pegs A to L.

19 Repeat steps 14 through 17, laying single bands in exactly the same way (except for band 1 on step 14, which should be an orange band this time), and then hook them in exactly the same way so that you have two layers of hooked hexagon.

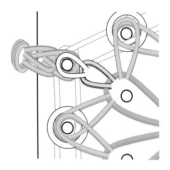

20 To make the top part of the shell pop up, it needs to be bigger than the underside. So pick up one of the white bands laid out in step 18 with your hook so that it loops through the colored loop beneath it.

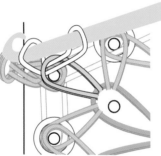

21 Then pull the colored loop off the peg and attach the white loops on your hook to the peg instead. Repeat all the way around the hexagon.

22 Hook the outer white bands laid out in step 13 in the order shown, to hold the two parts of the shell together.

23 Insert your hook into the top peg where the shell and the head meet, and gently pull the turtle off the loom.

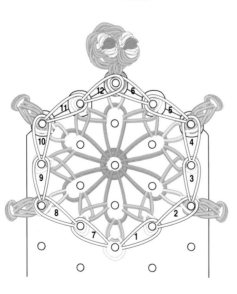

24 Thread a single white band through all the loops on your hook, going through the body and neck, and then insert one end of the white band through the other end. Pull tight to secure. To create the tail, pull the jade band out from the under-shell and tie a knot in it.

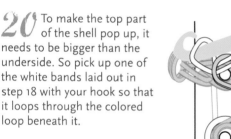
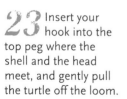

rockin' rooster

SKILL LEVEL ★

You Will Need

Loom

2 light orange bands

34 brown bands

7 yellow bands

6 dark orange bands

5 red bands

3 green bands

Hook

Holding hooks

You'll never forget to buy eggs again! This rooster magnet will be a great addition to the fridge; use it to hold favorite photos, notes, and shopping lists in place.

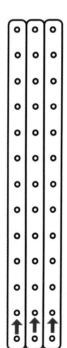

LOOM SETUP

Set up your loom in the square format—3 pegs wide x 13 pegs long (see page 6).

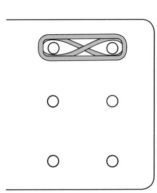

1 First make the feet. Take a light orange band and twist it once around two pegs in a figure-eight, then twist it again at one end and place it over the first peg.

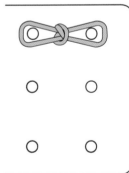

2 Using your hook, pick up the bottom right part of the band.

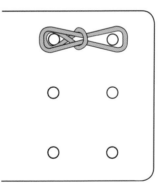

3 Hook it over the right peg into the center.

4 Repeat steps 2 and 3 on the left side to make a knot. Make another foot by repeating steps 1–4, then put the feet to one side.

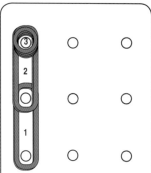

5 Now make the wing. With the arrows on the loom pointing away from you, lay out two pairs of brown bands, as shown. Add a brown cap band to the top band, twisting it around the peg four times.

6 Turn the loom around. Insert your hook into the bottom peg, under the cap band, pick up the two loops, and hook them over their opposing peg. Repeat on the next peg up.

7 Insert your hook into the top peg, through all the loops, and gently pull the wing off the loom, leaving it on the hook. Put to one side.

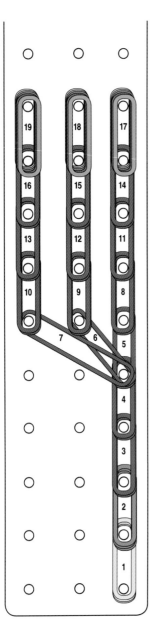
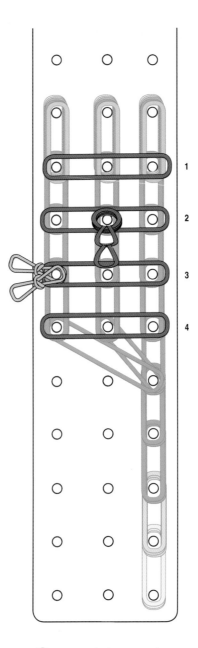
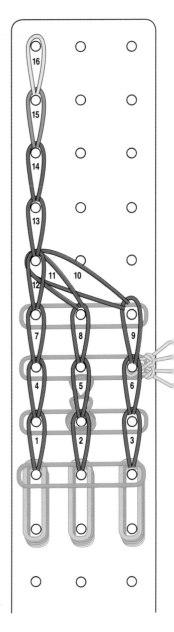

8 Now make the body. With the arrows on the loom pointing away from you, lay out pairs of bands in the order shown, except for bands 1 and 2, which are sets of three bands, and bands 5, 6, and 7, which are single bands. Bands 17, 18, and 19 are each made up from a yellow, dark orange, red, and green band.

9 Lay single horizontal brown bands over rows 2 and 3. Lay doubled-over single brown bands on rows 1 and 4. Lay the wing you made in steps 5–7 on the center peg of row 2. Finally, lay the feet you made in steps 1–4 on the outer left peg of row 3.

10 Turn the loom around. Starting from the bottom pairs of brown bands, hook the bands over their opposing pegs in the order shown. This will trap the feet, wing, and tail feathers in place.

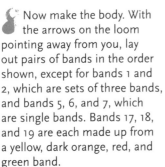

cute pets and furry friends

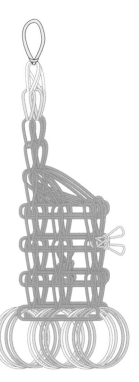

With the help of an adult, attach a magnet to the back of the rooster using a glue gun or Superglue, so it can live on your refrigerator!

11 Insert your hook into the top peg, through all the loops, and gently pull the rooster off the loom. Thread a single yellow band through all the loops on your hook, thread one end of the band through the other, and pull tight to secure.

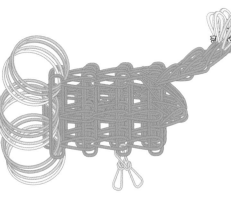

12 Using your hook, pull the single yellow band through the loops of the neck to bend the head over and create a beak.

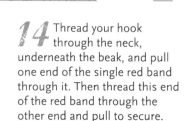

13 To make the wattle, wrap a single red band around your hook four times and pull another single red band through all the loops.

14 Thread your hook through the neck, underneath the beak, and pull one end of the single red band through it. Then thread this end of the red band through the other end and pull to secure.

15 Loop the remaining red loop over the wattle to neaten and complete it.

Neigh! Create your own cute pony charm. Ideal for horse and pony lovers, the loopy mane is particularly cool!

pippa the pony

You Will Need

Loom

162 turquoise bands

18 clear bands

8 gray bands

2 black bands

2 white bands

87 pink bands

Hook

Holding hooks

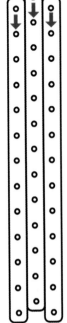

LOOM SETUP

Set up your loom in the diagonal format—3 pegs wide x 13 pegs long (see page 6).

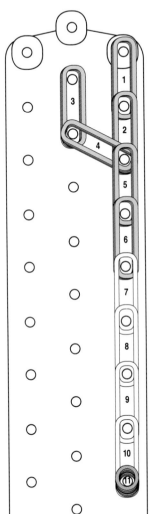

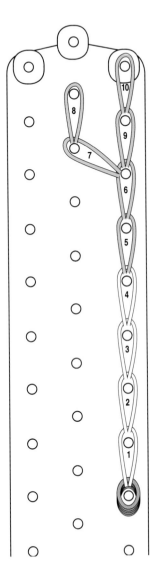

1 First make the hind legs. With the arrows on the loom pointing toward you, lay out sets of three turquoise bands and doubled-over single clear bands in the order shown. Add two gray cap bands to the bottom peg, twisting them around the peg three times.

2 Insert your hook into the bottom peg, under the cap bands, and hook the bands over their opposing pegs in the order shown.

3 Insert your holding hook into the top peg, through all the loops, and gently pull the leg off the loom, leaving it on the hook. Put to one side.

4 Repeat steps 1–3 to make a second hind leg.

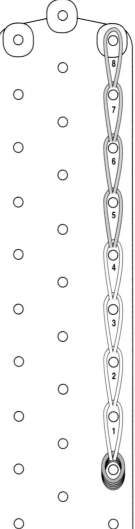

5 Now make the front legs. With the arrows on the loom pointing toward you, lay out sets of three turquoise bands and doubled-over single clear bands in the order shown. Add two gray cap bands to the bottom peg, twisting them around the peg three times.

6 Insert your hook into the bottom peg, under the cap bands, and hook the bands over their opposing pegs in the order shown.

7 Insert your holding hook into the top peg, through all the loops, and gently pull the leg off the loom, leaving it on the hook. Put to one side. Repeat steps 5–7 to make a second front leg.

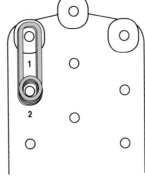

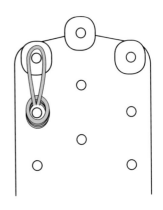

8 To make the ears, lay two turquoise bands between two pegs and place a turquoise cap band on the bottom peg, twisting it around the peg four times.

9 Insert your hook into the bottom peg, under the cap band, and hook the bands over the opposing peg.

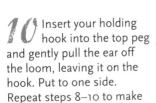

10 Insert your holding hook into the top peg and gently pull the ear off the loom, leaving it on the hook. Put to one side. Repeat steps 8–10 to make a second ear.

11 To make the eyes, wrap a black band around your hook four times, then pull a doubled-over single white band through the loops on the hook. Repeat with another black and white band. Pull a single turquoise band through all the loops on your hook, leaving it on the hook, and put to one side.

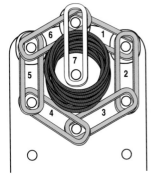

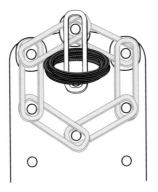

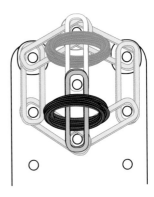

12 Now begin laying out the bands for the head. With the arrows on the loom pointing toward you, lay out pairs of turquoise bands in a hexagon. Then place ten pink bands on the center peg. Finally, place two clear bands between the top and center pegs of the hexagon.

13 Using your hook, pull the pink loops up over the center peg and onto the clear bands between the pegs.

14 Place ten more pink bands on the bottom peg of the hexagon, then lay two more turquoise bands on top. Using your hook, pull the pink bands up over the peg and onto the turquoise bands, as in step 13.

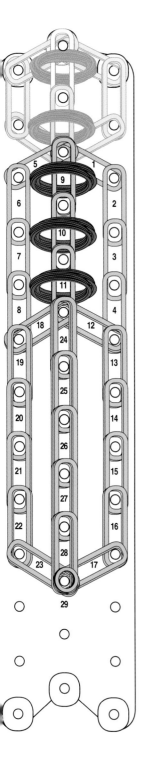

15 Continue laying turquoise bands to create the body. Bands 1 to 8 are single bands, bands 12 to 23 are pairs, and bands 24 to 28 are sets of three bands. Work bands 9 to 11 in the same way as the head, by placing ten pink bands on the lower peg with two turquoise bands over them, and hooking the pink bands onto the turquoise ones. Finally, add a turquoise cap band to the bottom peg, twisting it around the peg four times.

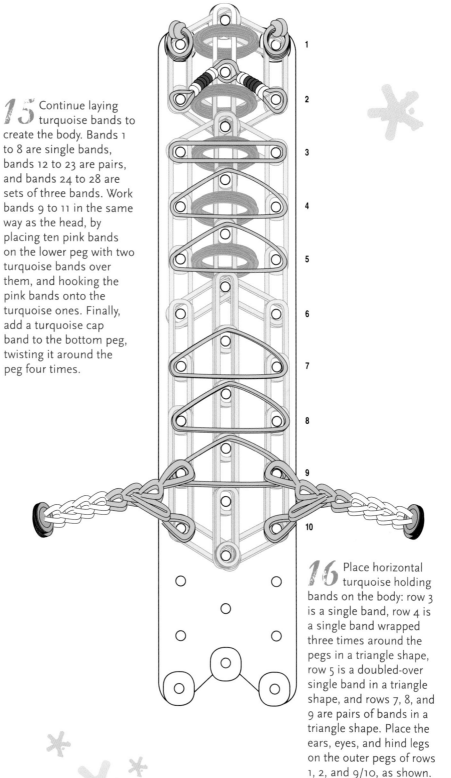

16 Place horizontal turquoise holding bands on the body: row 3 is a single band, row 4 is a single band wrapped three times around the pegs in a triangle shape, row 5 is a doubled-over single band in a triangle shape, and rows 7, 8, and 9 are pairs of bands in a triangle shape. Place the ears, eyes, and hind legs on the outer pegs of rows 1, 2, and 9/10, as shown.

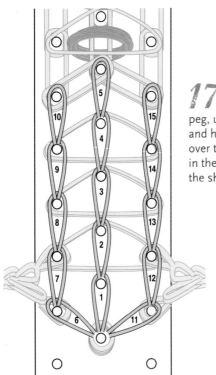

17 Insert your hook into the bottom peg, under the cap band, and hook the body bands over their opposing pegs in the order shown, up to the shoulders.

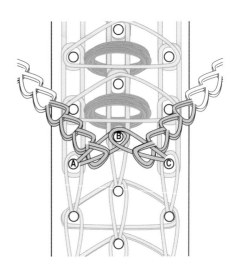

18 Now attach the front legs: thread one of the front legs onto your hook, insert it into peg A, pick up the bands on peg A, and thread the leg onto those loops. Then hook the loops onto peg B. Repeat with the other leg on pegs C and B.

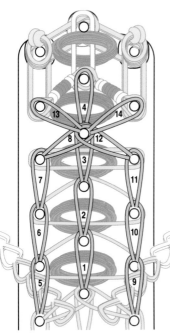

19 Hook the rest of the neck and lower face over their opposing pegs in the order shown.

20 Now make the muzzle, laying out bands in the order shown. Bands 1, 2, 3, 4, and 7 are pairs of turquoise bands; bands 5, 6, 8, and 9 are doubled-over single bands; band 10 is a doubled-over single band in a triangle shape; and band 11 is a horizontal doubled-over single. Add a turquoise cap band to the bottom center peg, twisting it around the peg four times.

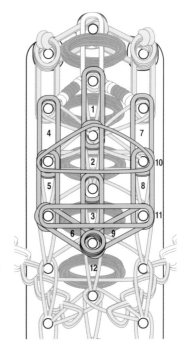

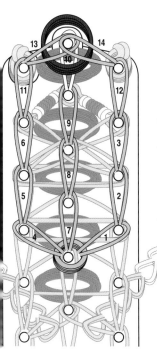

21 Insert your hook under the cap band and hook the bands in the order shown. Stop at band 12, place four pink bands in the top peg, and then hook bands 13 and 14; this creates the tuft of hair at the top of the head.

22 Insert your hook into the top peg, through all the loops, and gently pull the pony off the loom. Thread a single turquoise band through all the loops on your hook, thread one end of the band through the other, and pull tight to secure.

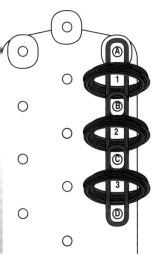

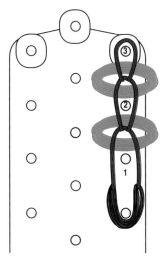

23 Now make the tail. Place ten pink bands on peg A, then place a single pink band over pegs A and B, and pull the loops onto the band. Repeat, placing ten pink bands on peg C and a single band over pegs B and C; then repeat once more, placing ten pink bands on peg D and a single band over pegs C and D.

24 Starting from the bottom, hook the single bands over their opposing pegs in the order shown.

25 Insert your hook into the top peg and gently pull the tail off the loom.

26 Insert your hook into the bottom of the pony and pull one of the pink loops through. Thread one of the pink bands through the other and pull tight to secure. Thread the remaining band back over the tail to secure.

A must-loop for any cat lover! Once you have mastered the technique, you can create your own pet in loops and then make it a little ball of wool to play with!

lola the cat

SKILL LEVEL ★★

You Will Need

Loom

69 dark gray bands

2 black bands

2 green bands

36 light gray bands

3 pink bands

18 white bands

Approx. 30 turquoise bands for ball of wool (optional)

Hook

Holding hooks

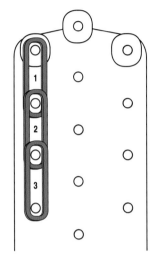

1 First, make the legs. With the arrow of the loom pointing toward you, lay out three pairs of dark gray bands in the order shown.

2 Wrap three light gray bands around your hook four times, so there are 12 loops on your hook. Pull a doubled-over single light gray band through all the loops on your hook.

LOOM SETUP

Set up your loom in the diagonal format— 3 pegs wide x 13 pegs long (see page 6).

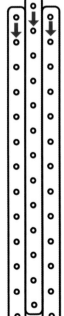

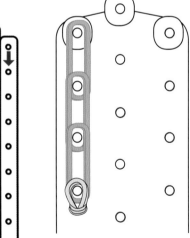

3 Place all end loops of the paw you have just made on the bottom peg of the leg, with the twists facing outward.

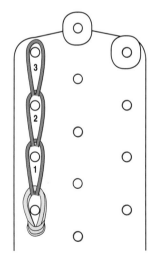

4 Insert your hook into the bottom peg, under the paw. Pick up the two dark gray bands and hook them over the peg above. Repeat with the remaining bands.

  cute pets and furry friends

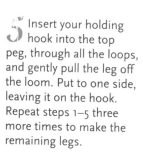

5 Insert your holding hook into the top peg, through all the loops, and gently pull the leg off the loom. Put to one side, leaving it on the hook. Repeat steps 1–5 three more times to make the remaining legs.

6 To make the eyes, wrap a black band around your hook four times and then pull a doubled-over single green band through all the loops on your hook. Repeat with another black and green band. Then pull a single light gray band through all the loops on your hook. Put to one side, leaving the eyes on the hook.

7 To make the nose, wrap a single pink band around your hook four times. Pull two doubled-over light gray bands through the pink loops. Then pull a single light gray band through all the loops on the hook. Put to one side, leaving it on the hook.

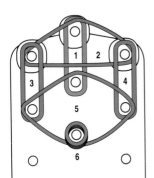

Now make the ears, placing bands over the pegs in the order shown. Band 1 is a single pink band, band 2 is a single dark gray band, and bands 3, 4, and 5 are doubled-over single dark gray bands. Add a dark gray cap band to the bottom peg, twisting it around the peg four times.

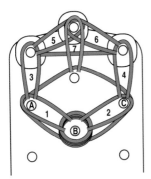

Insert your hook under the cap band (B), pick up the top loop of the doubled-over dark gray band, and hook it over peg A. Then go back into peg B, pick up the bottom loop of the doubled-over dark gray band, and hook it over peg C. Continue hooking the bands in the order shown, being very careful as the tension in the bands is very high.

10 Insert your hook into the top peg, through all the loops, gently pull the ear off the loom, and put it to one side, leaving it on the hook. Repeat steps 8–10 to make a second ear.

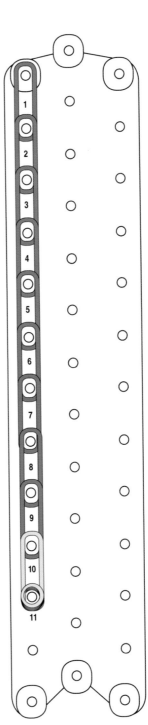

11 To make the tail, place doubled-over single bands in the order shown, except for band 1, which is a single band, and band 11, which is a single band twisted around the peg four times (that is, a cap band). Bands 1–9 are dark gray; bands 10 and 11 are light gray.

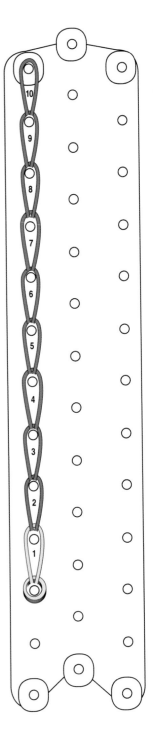

12 Insert your hook into the bottom peg and hook the bands over their opposing pegs in the order shown.

13 Insert your holding hook into the top peg and pull the tail gently off the loom. Put the tail to one side, leaving it on the hook.

14 Now make the body. With the arrows on the loom pointing toward you, lay out pairs of bands in the order shown. Bands 3, 7, 9, 13, 18, and 24 are light gray; bands 4, 8, 10, 11, 12, 17, 22, and 23 are white; and the rest are dark gray. Add a dark gray cap band to the bottom center peg, twisting it around the peg four times.

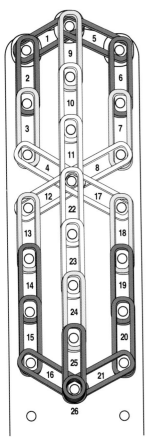

15 Add the ears, eyes, nose, and back legs to the body as shown. Place single horizontal light gray holding bands in a triangle shape over rows 2 and 3, and dark gray ones over rows 5 and 6.

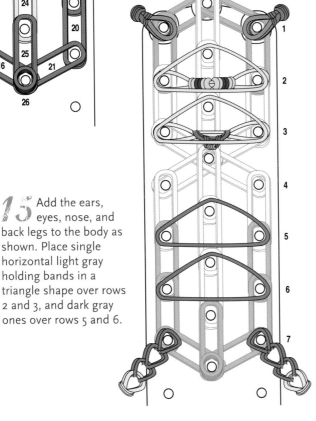

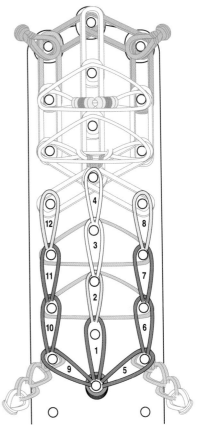

16 Starting from the bottom center peg, insert your hook, pick up the bottom two bands, and hook over the opposing peg. Repeat up to the shoulders in the order shown.

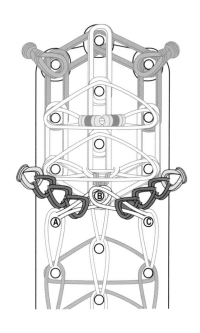

17 Thread the loops of one of the front legs onto your hook, insert the hook into peg A, pick up the two bands, and, before you hook them onto peg B, slide the leg onto the bands. Repeat with the remaining front leg on the bands between pegs B and C.

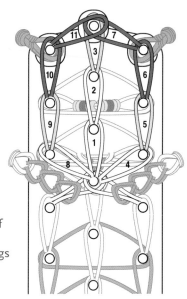

18 Hook the rest of the head bands over their opposing pegs in the order shown.

19 Insert your hook into the top peg through all the loops and gently pull the cat off the loom. Thread a single dark gray band through the loops on your hook. Thread one end through the other and pull to secure.

20 Attach the tail by threading your hook through the back of the cat and pulling the loops of the tail through.

21 Thread the tail through the loops on the hook and pull tight to secure.

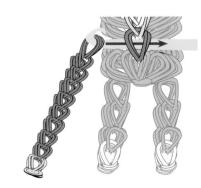

22 Insert your hook into the cat's muzzle and pull through two white bands. Cut the ends to make them into whiskers. The friction of the rubber keeps them in place.

23 To make the ball of wool, knot a few bands and then start wrapping individual bands over the knot until you have a ball approximately $1/2$ in. (1 cm) in diameter. Cut a single band in half and tie it to the ball to make the single string.

silly sausage dog

Sausage dogs are so popular at the moment! Follow these step-by-step instructions to create your very own rubber-band pet, then make him a cute little bone!

To make the sausage dog

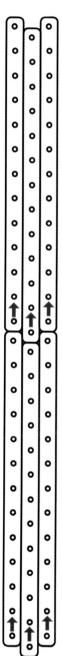

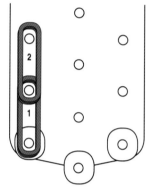

SKILL LEVEL ★ ★ ★

You Will Need

2 looms

86 brown bands

136 black bands

2 blue bands

21 white bands

2 blue bands

2 pink bands

2 jade bands

Hook

Holding hooks

1 Start by making the legs. With the arrows on the loom pointing away from you, lay out three brown bands between each pair of pegs, as shown.

2 Take a single brown band and wrap it around your hook four times. Take another single brown band, double it, and pull it through the loops on your hook.

3 Repeat step 2 two more times so you have 3 toes on your hook.

4 Pull a doubled single brown band through all the loops on your hook. This completes the foot.

LOOM SETUP

Set up your loom in the diagonal format—3 pegs wide x 26 pegs long (see page 6). You will need to join two looms together lengthwise.

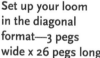

5 Place both end loops of the foot on the top peg of the leg you laid out in step 1.

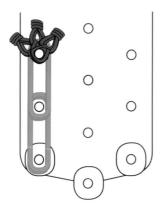

6 Turn the loom around, insert your hook into the bottom peg, pick up the bottom three bands, and hook them over the peg above. Then hook the remaining bands on the loom.

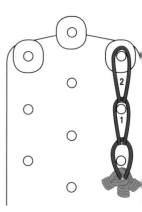

7 Insert your holding hook into the top peg, gently pull the leg off the loom, and put it to one side, leaving it on the hook. Repeat steps 1–7 three more times to make the rest of the legs.

8 Now make the ears. With the arrows on the loom pointing away from you, lay one black band on the bottom peg, then two on the next two pegs, and three bands on the fourth peg. Add a black cap band to the top peg, twisting it around the peg four times.

9 Turn your loom around, insert your hook into the bottom peg under the cap band, pick up the bands, and hook them over their opposing pegs in the order shown.

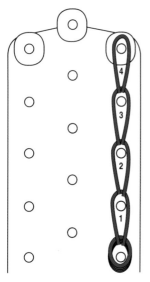

10 Insert your holding hook into the top peg and gently pull the ear off the loom. Put to one side, leaving it on the hook. Repeat steps 8–10 to make a second ear.

11 To make the eyes, twist a blue band around your hook four times, then pull a doubled-over white band through the blue bands. Repeat this with another white and blue band, then pull a single black band through all the loops on your hook and put to one side, leaving the eyes on the hook.

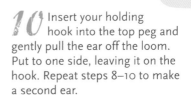

12 Now make the top of the muzzle. With the arrows on the loom pointing away from you, lay out pairs of bands in the order and colors shown.

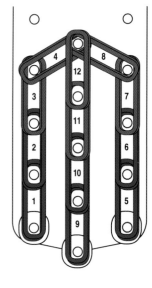

13 To make the nose, take a black band, wrap it around your hook four times, and pull a doubled-over black band through the loops. Put to one side, leaving it on the hook.

14 Place both loops of the nose you made in step 13 on the top peg of the bands laid out in step 12. Then lay two brown bands in a triangle shape over row 1, a doubled-over black band in a triangle shape over row 2, and a single black band in a triangle shape over row 3.

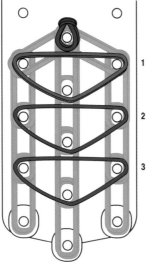

Use the loop at the top of the dog's head to hang him from a bag as a charm.

15 Turn the loom around. Starting from the bottom center band, hook the bands over their opposing pegs in the order shown.

16 Insert your holding hook into the top three pegs, through all the loops, and pull the muzzle piece gently off the loom. Put to one side, leaving it on the hook.

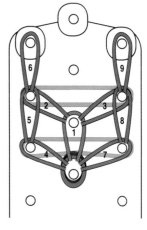

17 To make the lower jaw, with the arrows of the loom pointing away from you, lay out pairs of bands in the order shown, except for bands 11 and 12, which are single doubled-over bands, and band 10, which is a single band wrapped around the peg four times (that is, a cap band). All the bands in this step are brown, except for band 9, which is pink.

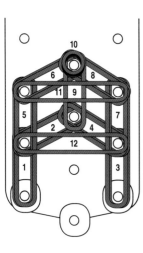

18 Turn the loom around and hook the bands over their opposing pegs in the order shown.

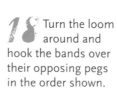

19 Insert your holding hook into the top pegs and pull the lower jaw gently off the loom. Put it to one side, leaving it on the hook.

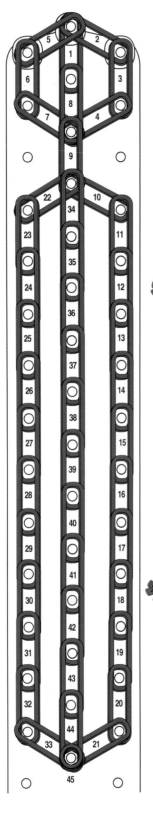

20 Now make the head and body. With the arrows on the loom pointing toward you, lay out pairs of black bands in the order shown. Add a black cap band to the bottom peg, twisting it around the peg four times.

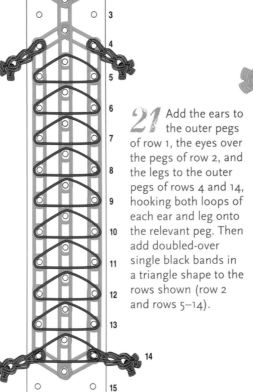

21 Add the ears to the outer pegs of row 1, the eyes over the pegs of row 2, and the legs to the outer pegs of rows 4 and 14, hooking both loops of each ear and leg onto the relevant peg. Then add doubled-over single black bands in a triangle shape to the rows shown (row 2 and rows 5–14).

22 Starting from the bottom peg, hook the bands over their opposing pegs up to the neck in the order shown. On move 36, insert your hook, pick up the two bands, and thread two jade bands through them to create the dog's collar before you hook them onto the opposing peg.

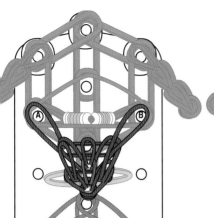

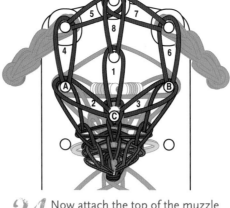

23 Attach the lower jaw made in steps 17–19 to the head by placing the four left loops on the left peg of the head (peg A) and the remaining four loops on the right peg of the head (peg B).

24 Now attach the top of the muzzle made in steps 14–16 to the loom by placing the four left loops on peg A, the next four on peg C, and the remaining four on peg B. Then hook the head bands over their opposing pegs in the order shown.

25 Insert your hook into the top peg and gently pull the dog off the loom. Thread a single black band through all the loops, thread one end of the band through the other, and pull tight to secure.

26 To make the tail, insert your hook into the back of the dog, pull a single brown band through, and thread one end through the other. Tie a knot in the top of the band to complete.

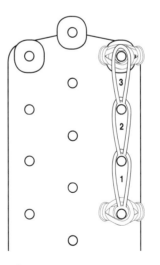

To make the bone

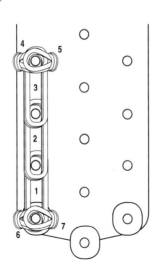

1 With the arrows on the loom pointing away from you, lay out three pairs of white bands in the order shown. For the knobbly bone ends, twist a white band around your hook four times and pull two white bands through the loops on your hook. Make three more of these, then lay two bone ends over the top peg and two over the bottom peg of the loom as shown, with the twists on the outer edge.

2 Turn the loom around and hook the bands over their opposing pegs in the order shown.

3 Insert your hook into the top peg, through all the loops, and gently pull the bone off the loom. Thread a single white band through all the loops, then thread one end of the band through the other. Pull tight to secure.

marnie the mouse

With her twitching whiskers and long tail, this little mouse would make an adorable charm to attach to your pencil case.

SKILL LEVEL ★★

You Will Need

2 looms

113 white bands

28 pink bands

2 blue bands

2 gray bands

Hook

Holding hooks

LOOM SETUP

Set up your loom in the diagonal format—3 pegs wide x 13 pegs long (see page 6). To make the tail (see step 10), you will have to join two looms together lengthwise.

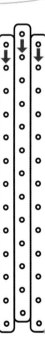

1 Start by making the ears. With the arrows on the loom pointing toward you, lay out pairs of white and pink bands in the order shown. Add a white cap band to the bottom peg, twisting it around the peg four times.

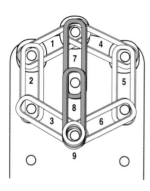

2 Add a pair of white bands in a triangle shape, as shown.

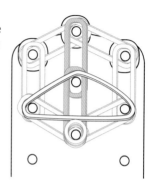

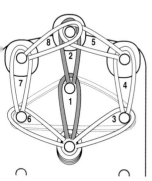

3 Starting from the bottom center peg, hook the bands over their opposing pegs in the order shown.

4 Insert your holding hook into the top peg, through all the loops, and gently pull the ear off the loom. Put to one side, leaving it on the hook. Repeat steps 1–4 to make a second ear.

5 To make the nose, wrap a pink band around your hook four times and pull two white bands through the loops. Pull a single white band through all the loops on your hook and put the nose to one side, leaving it on the hook.

6 To make the eyes, wrap a blue band around your hook four times, then pull a doubled-over white band through the black loops. Repeat with another blue and white band, then pull a single white band through all the loops on your hook and put the eyes to one side, leaving them on the hook.

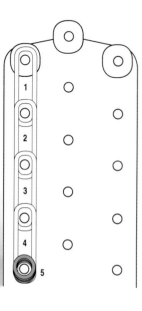

7 Now make the legs. With the arrows on the loom pointing toward you, lay out doubled-over single white bands in the order shown, then add a pink cap band to the bottom peg, twisting it around the peg four times.

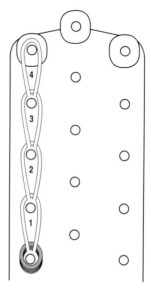

8 Insert your hook into the bottom peg and hook the bands over their opposing pegs in the order shown.

9 Insert your holding hook into the top peg and gently pull the leg off the loom. Put to one side. Repeat steps 7–9 to make three more legs. Note that I made the hind legs with five white bands instead of four.

10 To make the tail, repeat steps 7–9 but using 15 pink bands—that is, laying out 14 doubled-over single pink bands and then a pink cap band on the bottom peg. (Note that you will have to join two looms together lengthwise to make a 3 x 26-peg loom). Put the tail to one side, leaving it on the hook.

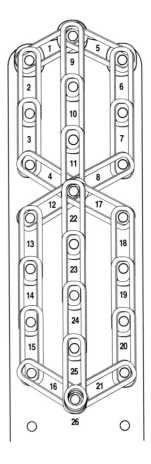

11 Now make the body. With the arrows on the loom pointing toward you, lay out pairs of white bands in the order shown. Add a white cap band to the bottom center peg, twisting it around the peg four times.

12 Add the ears, eyes, nose, and hind legs to the body as shown. Place the ears on the outer pegs of row 1, the eyes over row 2, the nose over row 3, and the hind legs on the outer pegs of row 7. Then place a single white holding band over row 1 and pairs of white bands in a triangle shape over rows 5, 6, and 7.

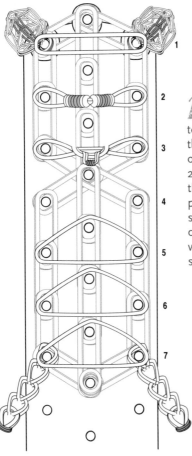

13 Starting from the bottom center peg, hook the bands over their opposing pegs in the order shown, up to the shoulders.

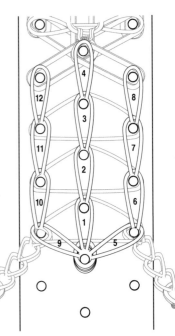

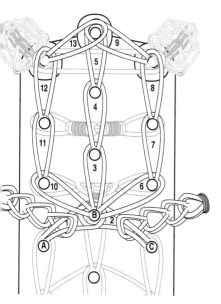

14 Thread the loops of one of the front legs onto your hook, insert the hook into peg A, pick up the two bands, and, before you hook them onto peg B, slide the leg onto the bands. Repeat with the remaining front leg on the bands between pegs B and C. Then hook the rest of the mouse in the order shown.

15 Insert your hook into the top peg and gently pull the mouse off the loom. Thread a single white band through all the loops on your hook, thread one end of the band through the other, and pull tight to secure.

To make a gray mouse, simply replace all the white bands with gray bands, except bands 4, 8, and 11 in step 11, which should be white. The eyes are made from black bands instead of blue.

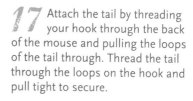

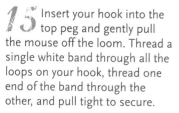

16 Using your hook, pull two gray bands through the nose of the mouse. The friction of the rubber bands will hold them in place. Cut the bands at each side to create whiskers.

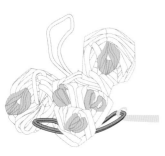

17 Attach the tail by threading your hook through the back of the mouse and pulling the loops of the tail through. Thread the tail through the loops on the hook and pull tight to secure.

Oink, oink! This cheerful little pig will brighten up a bag, purse, or pencil case no end. Attaching the head separately means he looks up, unlike many other animals in this book that look down.

pete the pig

SKILL LEVEL ★★

You Will Need

Loom

141 pink bands

11 black bands

2 white bands

Hook

Holding hooks

LOOM SETUP

Set up your loom in the diagonal format—3 pegs wide x 13 pegs long (see page 6).

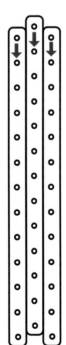

1 Start by making the legs. With the arrows on the loom pointing toward you, lay out three pink bands between each pair of pegs in the order shown. Add a cap band by twisting two black bands around the bottom peg four times.

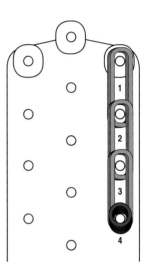

2 Insert your hook into the bottom peg, under the cap bands, and hook the bands over their opposing pegs in the order shown.

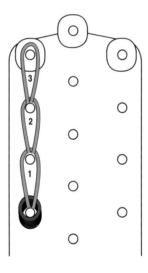

3 Insert your holding hook into the top peg, pull the leg gently off the loom, and put it to one side, leaving it on the hook. Repeat steps 1–3 three times to make three more legs.

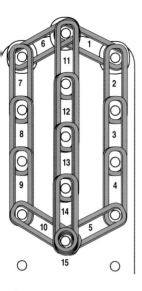

4 Now make the head. With the arrows on the loom pointing toward you, lay out pink bands in the order shown; they are all pairs, except bands 12, 13, and 14, which are three bands each. Add a pink cap band to the bottom center peg, twisting it around the peg four times.

5 To make the snout, wrap a black band around your hook four times, pull a pair of pink bands through the loops, then pull a single pink band through the pink loops. Put to one side, leaving it on the hook.

6 To make the eyes, wrap a black band around your hook three times, then wrap a white band around your hook three times. Repeat with another white and then another black band so that there are 12 loops on your hook. Pull a single pink band through all the loops on your hook and then put the eyes to one side, leaving them on the hook.

7 Now make the ears. Wrap a single pink band around your hook four times and then pull two pink bands through the loops on your hook. Repeat to make a second ear and put to one side, leaving the ears on the hook.

8 Place the ears, eyes, and snout on the head, as shown. Then add a doubled-over single pink holding band over row 1, a pair of pink bands in a triangle shape over row 3, and a doubled-over single pink band in a triangle shape over row 4.

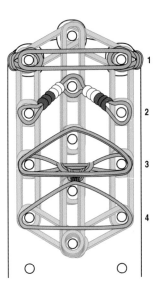

9 Starting from the bottom of the head, hook the bands over their opposing pegs in the order shown.

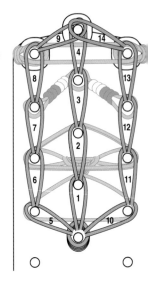

10 Insert your hook into the top peg and gently pull the head off the loom. Thread a single pink band through all the loops on your hook, and thread one end through the other to secure.

11 To emphasize the snout, wrap a pink band around it three times. Put the head to one side.

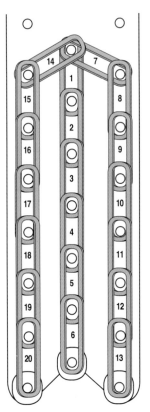

12 To make the body, with the arrows on the loom pointing toward you, lay out pairs of pink bands in the order shown.

13 Place a pair of pink horizontal holding bands over row 1, and pairs of pink holding bands in a triangle shape over rows 2–6. Hook the pair of holding bands on row 7 over the center peg rather than in a triangle shape, as shown. Then add the legs over the outer pegs of rows 1 and 7.

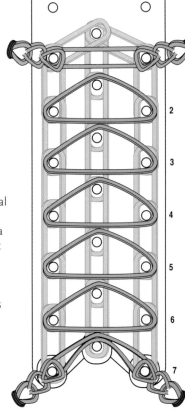

14 Insert your hook into the back left-hand side of the pig's head and pull a single pink band through. Repeat with another single pink band on the right-hand side.

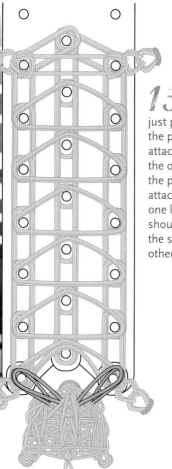

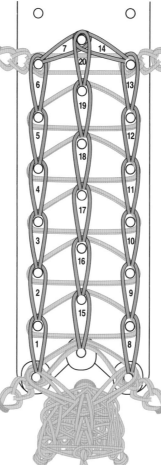

15 Using the loops you just pulled through the pig's head, attach the head to the outer pegs of the pig's shoulders: attach both ends of one loop onto one shoulder, then do the same with the other side.

16 Starting from the shoulders, hook the bands over their opposing pegs in the order shown.

17 Insert your hook into the top peg and gently pull the pig off the loom. Thread a single pink band through all the loops on your hook, then thread one end of the band through the other, and pull tight to secure.

friendly frog

This bright tropical frog would make a great magnet for holding favorite photos, pictures, and mementos.

SKILL LEVEL ★

You Will Need

Loom

17 pink jelly bands

37 orange bands

53 lime green bands

50 yellow jelly bands

4 blue bands or 2 pony beads

Hook

Holding hooks

Note: These quantities are for the frog with the yellow and lime green body; if you would prefer to make your frog with a pink and orange body, you will need 53 pink bands, 50 orange, 17 lime green, and 37 yellow.

LOOM SETUP

Set up your loom in the diagonal format—3 pegs wide x 13 pegs long (see page 6).

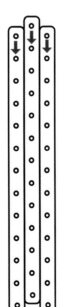

1 Start by making the arms. Wrap a pink band around your hook four times and then pull two orange bands through the loops.

2 Make two more "toes" in the same way as in step 1, then thread two orange bands through all the loops on your hook.

3 Take one yellow and one lime green band and pull these through the orange loops on your hook. Repeat with two more pairs of yellow and lime green bands.

4 Repeat steps 1–3 to make a second arm.

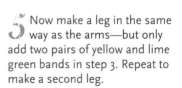

5 Now make a leg in the same way as the arms—but only add two pairs of yellow and lime green bands in step 3. Repeat to make a second leg.

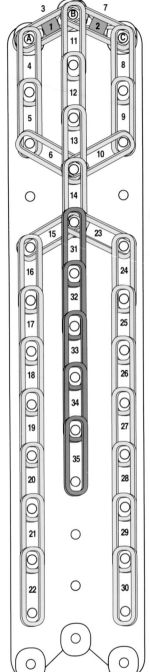

6 To make the eyes, either thread a single bead onto a yellow band or wrap two blue bands around your hook four times, then pull a single yellow band through these loops. Repeat to make a second eye and put to one side, leaving the eyes on the hook.

With the help of an adult, attach a magnet to the back of the frog using a glue gun or Superglue. Allow to cool before using.

7 Now make the frog's body and head. With the arrows on the loom pointing toward you, place one eye on pegs A and B, and the other eye on pegs B and C. Then lay out pairs of bands (made up of either one yellow and one lime green band, or one pink and one orange band) in the order shown. For the ridge down the frog's back (bands 31–35), reverse the colors—so if your frog's body is yellow and lime green, as here, make the ridge with pink and orange bands, and vice versa.

8 To make the frog's thighs, wrap a yellow band around your hook four times, then thread through four pairs of one lime green and one yellow band.

9 Place the loops on your hook on peg A and place the yellow cap band of the thigh piece on peg B.

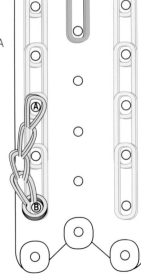

10 Repeat steps 8 and 9 to make and position the other thigh.

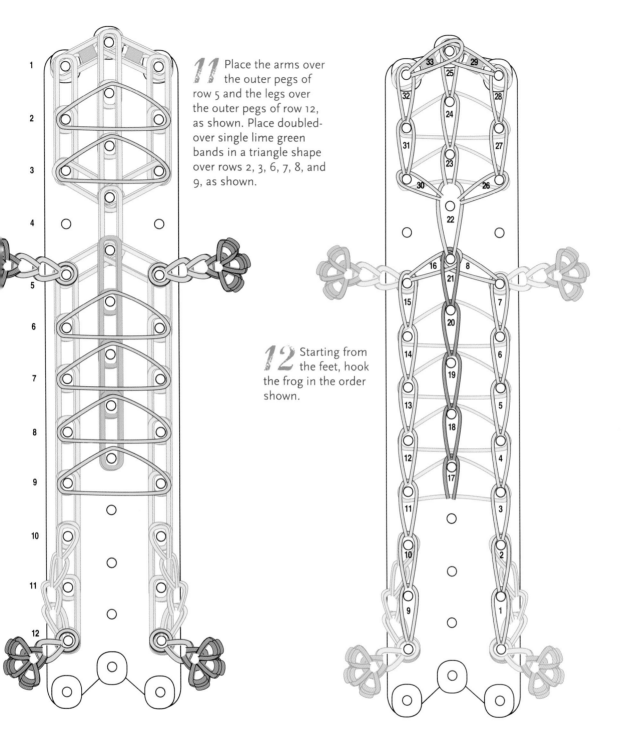

11 Place the arms over the outer pegs of row 5 and the legs over the outer pegs of row 12, as shown. Place doubled-over single lime green bands in a triangle shape over rows 2, 3, 6, 7, 8, and 9, as shown.

12 Starting from the feet, hook the frog in the order shown.

13 Insert your hook into the top peg and gently pull the frog off the loom. Thread a single lime green band through all the loops on your hook, thread one end of the band through the other, and pull tight to secure.

bunny and carrot bracelet

This is the perfect spring accessory! Why not try making several as Easter gifts?

Making the bunny

SKILL LEVEL ★★

You Will Need

- 2 looms
- 36 orange bands
- 18 green bands
- 83 purple bands
- 2 black bands
- 57 white bands
- 10 pink bands
- Hook
- Holding hooks
- C-clip

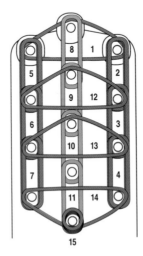

1 Start by making the bunny's ears. With the arrows on the loom pointing toward you, lay out bands in the colors and order shown. Bands 1, 8, 9, 10, and 11 are single bands; bands 12, 13, and 14 are doubled-over singles in a triangle shape; and the rest are pairs. Band 15 is a cap band twisted around the peg four times.

LOOM SETUP FOR THE BUNNY

Set up your loom in the diagonal format— 3 pegs wide x 13 pegs long (see page 6).

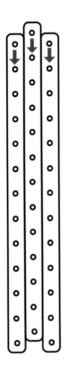

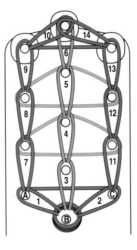

2 Insert your hook into peg B, pick up the top band of the doubled-over single band, and hook it over peg A. Then hook the lower band of the doubled band over peg C. Hook the rest of the bands as normal in the order shown.

3 Insert your holding hook into the top peg and gently pull the ear off the loom. Repeat steps 1–3 to make a second ear.

4 To make the eyes, wrap a black band around your hook four times and pull a doubled-over single white band through all the loops on your hook. Repeat with another black and white band. Then pull a single purple band through all the loops on your hook. Put to one side, leaving the eyes on the hook.

5 To make the nose, wrap a pink band around your hook four times and pull a doubled-over single pink band through all the loops on your hook. Then pull a single white band through all the loops on your hook. Put to one side, leaving the nose on the hook.

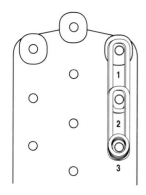

6 To make the cheeks, lay out pairs of white bands in the order shown. Add a white cap band to the bottom peg, twisting it around the peg four times.

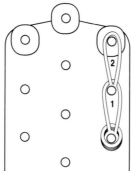

7 Insert your hook into the bottom peg and hook the bands over their opposing pegs in the order shown.

8 Insert your holding hook into the top peg and gently pull the cheek off the loom. Put it to one side, leaving it on the hook. Repeat steps 6–8 to make another cheek.

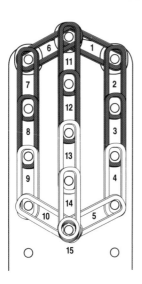

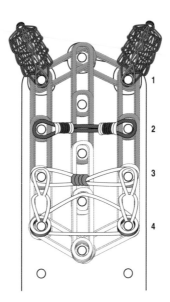

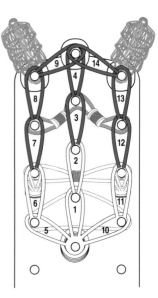

9 To make the rabbit's head, lay out pairs of bands in the colors and order shown. Add a white cap band to the bottom peg, twisting it around the peg four times.

10 Add a single white band in a triangle shape over row 4. Then add the ears to the outer pegs of row 1, the eyes over row 2, the nose over row 3, and the cheeks to the outer pegs of rows 3 and 4.

11 Starting from the bottom of the head, hook the bands over their opposing pegs in the order shown.

12 Insert your hook into the top peg and gently pull the head off the loom. Thread a single purple band through all the loops on your hook, then thread one end of the purple band through the other and pull tight to secure.

Making the carrot

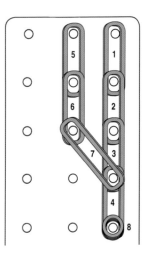

LOOM SETUP FOR THE CARROT

Set up your loom in the square format—
3 pegs wide x 13 pegs long (see page 6).

13 With the arrows on the loom pointing toward you, lay out pairs of orange bands in the order shown. Add a cap band to the bottom peg by twisting a single orange band around the peg four times.

14 To make the leaves, place three green bands on your hook, then pull a doubled-over single green band through the loops.

15 Thread one end of the doubled-over green band through the other, and pull tight to secure. Repeat steps 14 and 15 to make a second set of leaves.

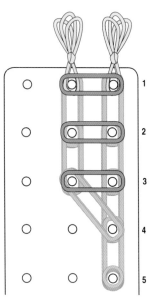

16 Place one leaf on each of the top two pegs of the carrot, twisting the loops around the peg twice. Then place doubled-over single orange bands on rows 1, 2, and 3.

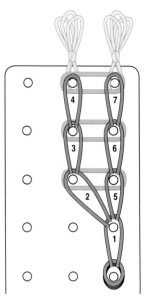

17 Starting at the cap band, hook the bands over their opposing pegs in the order shown.

18 Insert your hook into the top two pegs of the carrot, through all the loops, and gently pull the carrot off the loom. Thread a single green band through all the loops on your hook and thread one end through the other to secure. Repeat steps 13–18 to make a second carrot.

Making the bracelet

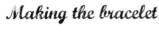

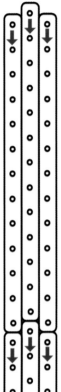

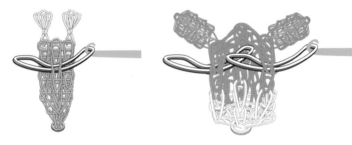

19 Thread a pair of one white and one purple band through the backs of both of the carrots, then thread two pairs of white and purple bands through the back of the bunny's head.

LOOM SETUP FOR THE BRACELET

Set up your loom in the diagonal format— 3 pegs wide x 26 pegs long (see page 6). You will need to join two looms together lengthwise.

20 With the arrows on the loom pointing toward you, lay out pairs of one white and one purple band all the way along it. Add a purple cap band to the bottom peg, twisting it around the peg four times.

26

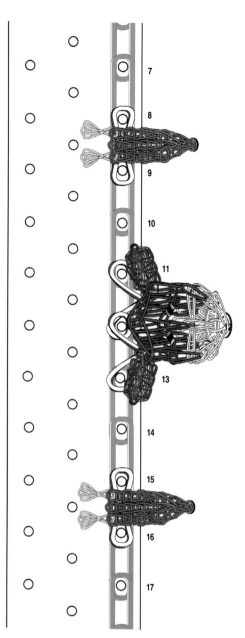

7

8

9

10

11

12

13

14

15

16

17

21 Place the carrots over the pegs on rows 8 and 9, and 15 and 16. Then add the loops of the bunny's head between pegs 11 and 12, and 12 and 13.

25
24
23
22
21
20
19
18
17
16
15
14
13
12
11
10
9
8
7
6
5
4
3
2
1

22 Starting from the cap band at the bottom, loop the bands over their opposing pegs in the order shown. This will trap the charms in place on the bracelet.

23 Insert a C-clip through the bands at the top of the loom and gently pull the bracelet off the loom. Thread the cap band loops through the C-clip, too, to close the bracelet.

tropical fish

Create a shoal of tropical fish using this loopy fish pattern. They are 3-D, too, which is even cooler!

SKILL LEVEL ★★★

You Will Need

Loom

44 red bands

2 black bands

2 white bands

81 green bands

7 orange bands

1 pink band

Hook

Holding hooks

LOOM SETUP

Set up your loom in the diagonal format—3 pegs wide x 13 pegs long (see page 6).

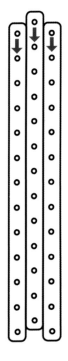

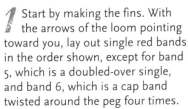

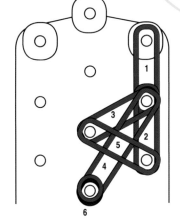

1 Start by making the fins. With the arrows of the loom pointing toward you, lay out single red bands in the order shown, except for band 5, which is a doubled-over single, and band 6, which is a cap band twisted around the peg four times.

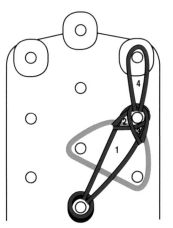

2 Starting at the cap band, hook the bands over their opposing pegs in the order shown.

3 Insert your holding hook into the top peg and gently pull the fin off the loom. Put to one side, leaving the fin on the hook. Repeat steps 1–3 to make a second fin.

4 To make the eyes, wrap a black band around your hook four times and pull a doubled-over single white band through all the loops on your hook. Repeat with another black and white band. Then pull a single green band through all the loops on your hook. Put to one side, leaving the eyes on the hook.

5 To make the tongue, tie a pink band in half.

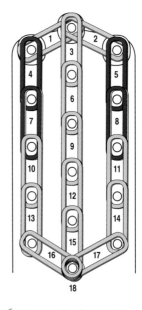

6 Now make the head. Lay out pairs of bands in the colors and order shown. Note that bands 7 and 8 are made up of one red and one green band. Add a green cap band to the bottom peg, twisting it around the peg four times.

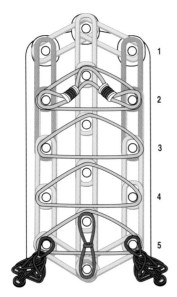

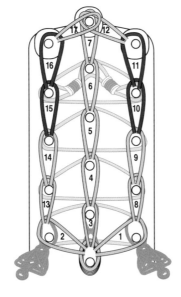

7 Place a doubled-over single green holding band in a triangle shape over row 2, and single green holding bands in a triangle shape over rows 3–5. Then add the eyes, tongue, and fins in the positions shown.

8 Hook the bands over their opposing pegs in the order shown.

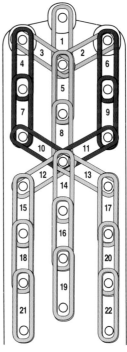

9 Insert your hook into the top peg and gently pull the head off the loom. Thread two red bands through the loops on your hook, then thread one end of the red bands through the other and pull tight to secure. Put to one side.

10 Now make the body and tail. With the arrows on the loom pointing toward you, lay out pairs of bands in the colors and order shown, except for bands 1, 2, 3, 8, 10, 11, 12, 13, and 14, which are singles.

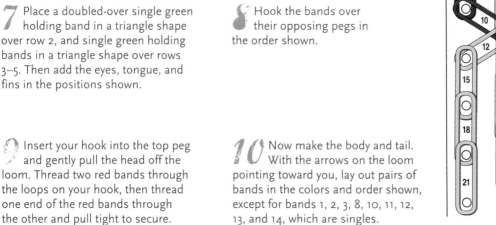

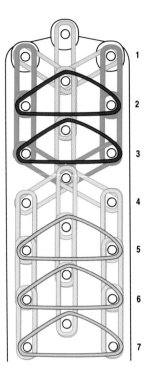

11 Place horizontal holding bands in a triangle shape over rows 2, 3, 5, 6, and 7, in the colors shown. They are all singles except for row 3, which is a doubled-over single.

12 To make the tail more pointed, you need extra tail pieces. Wrap a red band around your hook four times and pull a doubled single red band through the loops. Put to one side, leaving it on the hook. Repeat to make a second tail piece.

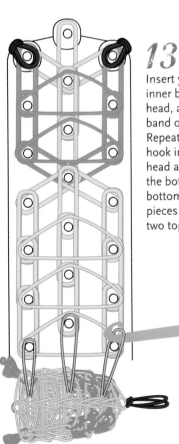

13 Before hooking the bands, you need to attach the head. Insert your hook into one of the inner bands on one side of the head, above the fin. Place that band on the bottom left peg. Repeat twice more, inserting your hook into the same side of the head and hooking the loops onto the bottom center and then the bottom right peg. Then add the tail pieces you made in step 12 to the two top outer pegs.

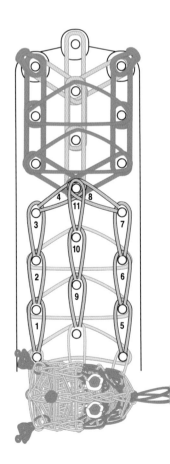

14 Hook the bands over their opposing pegs in the order shown up to the tail, and then stop!

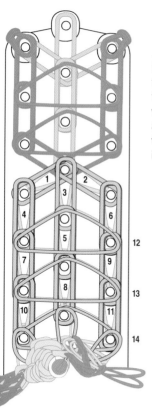

15 Lay out another layer of green bands in the order shown; they are all pairs, except for bands 1, 2, and 3, which are singles. Then attach the other side of the fish's head as you did in step 13.

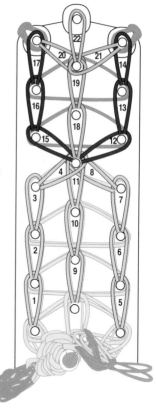

16 Hook the bands over their opposing pegs in the order shown.

17 Insert your hook into the top peg and pull the fish gently off the loom. Thread a single orange band through all the loops on your hook, then thread one end through the other and pull tight to secure.

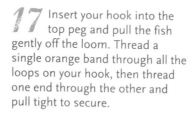

18 To "sew" the top of the fish together and create the stripes, insert your hook into the top bands of the body near the head and pull a single red band through.

19 Thread your hook through one end of the band you have just pulled through, then through both loops on the top of the fish's head, and then through the other end of the red band. Pull another single red band through all these loops.

20 Now thread one of the ends through the other to secure all the bands on it.

21 Repeat steps 18–20 three more times along the rest of the fish, using the loop from the previous stitch to pull through each time. By inserting your hook through the middle of the fish rather than through the top loops, you create a striped pattern.

Farm your own flock of sheep! Make fluffy sheep with loopy coats for a fun looping project.

barry the sheep

SKILL LEVEL ★ ★

You Will Need

Loom

168 white bands

11 black bands

1 pink band

26 gray bands

Hook

Holding hooks

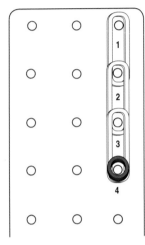

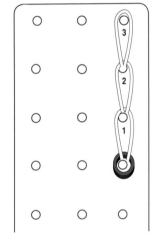

LOOM SETUP

Set up your loom in the square format—3 pegs wide x 13 pegs long (see page 6).

1 Start by making the legs. With the arrows on the loom pointing toward you, lay out pairs of white bands in the order shown. Add two black cap bands to the bottom peg by twisting them around the peg four times.

2 Starting at the cap band, hook the bands over their opposing pegs in the order shown.

3 Insert your holding hook into the top peg and gently pull the leg off the loom. Put the leg to one side, leaving it on the hook. Repeat steps 1–3 to make three more legs in the same way.

4 To make the eyes, wrap a black band around your hook four times and pull a doubled-over single white band through all the loops on your hook. Repeat with another black and white band. Then pull a single white band through all the loops on your hook. Put the eyes to one side, leaving them on the hook.

cute pets and furry friends

5 To make the nose, wrap a single pink band around your hook four times and then pull a doubled-over single gray band through all the loops on your hook. Then pull a single gray band through all the loops on your hook.

6 To make the ears, wrap a gray band around your hook four times and pull two white bands through them. Put to one side, leaving the ear on the hook. Repeat to make a second ear.

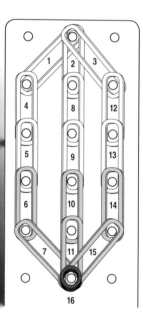

7 To make the head, with the arrows on the loom pointing toward you, lay out pairs of bands in the colors and order shown. Add a black cap band to the bottom peg, twisting it around the peg four times.

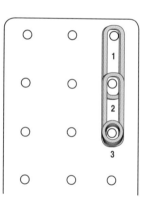

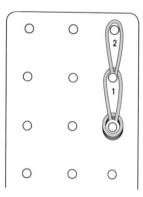

8 To make the cheeks, lay pairs of gray bands in the order shown. Add a gray cap band to the bottom peg, twisting it around the peg four times.

9 Hook the bands over their opposing pegs in the order shown, then insert your holding hook into the top band and gently pull the cheek off the loom. Put to one side, leaving the cheek on the hook. Repeat steps 8 and 9 to make a second cheek.

10 Place the ears on row 2, eyes on row 3, nose on row 5, and cheeks on rows 5 and 6, hooking the cap bands of each cheek onto peg A. Then add a single horizontal white holding band over row 2 and a doubled-over single white band on row 4.

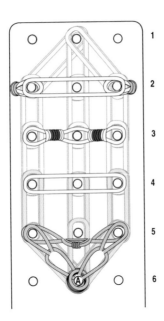

	1
	2
	3
	4
	5
	6

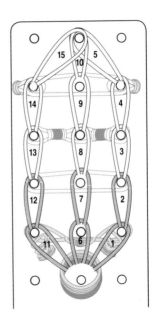

11 Starting from the cap band, hook the bands over their opposing pegs in the order shown.

12 Insert your hook into the top peg and gently pull the head off the loom. Thread three white bands through the loops on your hook, then thread one set of ends through the other to secure.

13 With the arrows on the loom pointing toward you, place four white bands on each peg, as shown.

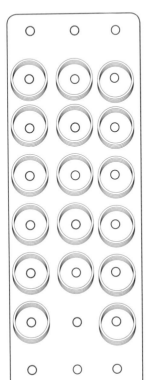

14 Place a pair of white bands diagonally on the loom, as shown. Using your hook, pull the four bands that were on the left-hand peg of the first row up and onto the pair of white bands.

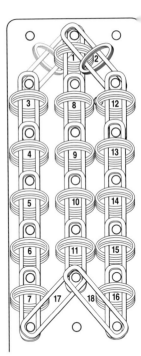

15 Continue placing pairs of bands on the pegs and then pulling the sets of four loose bands up and onto the pairs. Bands 17 and 18 are pairs of white bands without any loose bands to pull onto them.

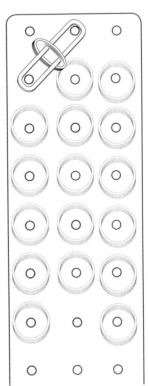

16 Insert your hook into the back of the sheep's head and pull two white bands through near the base of the head.

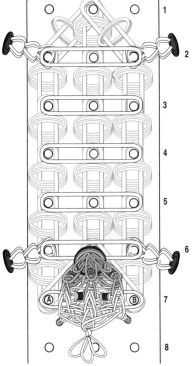

17 Place the head upside down on the loom and place the loops of the bands you just attached in step 16 on pegs A and B on row 7. Add the legs to the outer pegs of rows 2 and 6. Place doubled-over single white horizontal holding bands over rows 2–6, as shown.

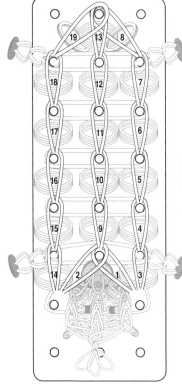

18 Hook the bands over their opposing pegs in the order shown.

19 Insert your hook into the top peg and pull the sheep off the loom. Thread a single white band through the loops on your hook, then thread one end through the other and pull tight to secure.

chapter 2

into the *wild*

percy the penguin

You'll be so cool with this funky penguin brooch.
Try making it in black, silver, or even purple bands.

SKILL LEVEL ★

You Will Need

Loom

57 black bands

27 white bands

14 orange bands

2 blue bands

Hook

Holding hooks

LOOM SETUP

Set up your loom
in the diagonal
format—3 pegs
wide x 13 pegs long
(see page 6).

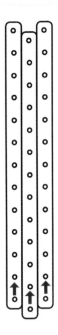

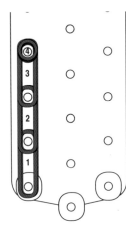

1 Start by making the
wings. With the arrows
on the loom pointing away
from you, lay out pairs of
black bands in the order
shown. Add a black cap
band to the top peg, twisting
it around the peg four times.

2 Turn the loom around.
Insert your hook into the
bottom peg, under the cap
band, and hook the bands over
their opposing pegs in the
order shown.

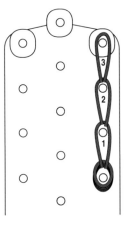

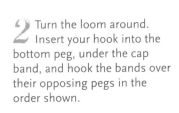

3 Insert your holding hook into the
top peg, through all the loops, and
gently pull the wing off the loom, leaving
it on the hook. Put to one side. Repeat
steps 1–3 to make a second wing.

4 Now make the beak. With the
arrows on the loom pointing away
from you, lay a doubled-over single
orange band over two pegs. Add an
orange cap band to the top peg, twisting
it around the peg four times.

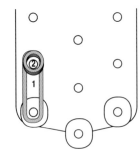

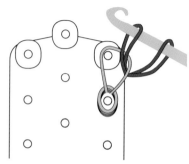

5 Turn the loom around. Insert your hook into the bottom peg, under the cap band, and hook the band over its opposing peg. Thread a single black band through the loops on the peg.

6 Pull the beak gently off the loom and place it on a holding hook. Put to one side.

7 To make the feet, twist a single orange band around your hook three times. Then repeat twice more so that you have nine loops on your hook.

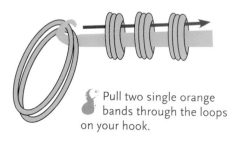

8 Pull two single orange bands through the loops on your hook.

9 Twist another orange band around your hook three times and pull two black bands through the loops.

10 Now pull the right-hand set of black bands through both sets of orange bands on the hook, so that the second bunch of orange bands sits above the first. Repeat steps 7–10 to make a second foot.

11 To make the eyes, wrap a white band around your hook twice, then wrap a blue band around it four times, then wrap the original white band around the hook twice more. Repeat with another white and blue band to make the second eye.

12 Pull a single black band through all the loops on your hook and place on a holding hook. Put to one side.

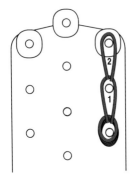

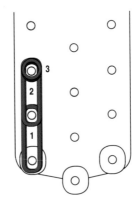

13 Now make the tail. With the arrows on the loom pointing away from you, lay out two pairs of black bands in the order shown. Add a black cap band to the top peg, twisting it around the peg four times.

14 Turn the loom around. Insert your hook into the bottom peg, under the cap band, and hook the bands over their opposing pegs in the order shown.

15 Insert your holding hook into the top peg, through all the loops, and gently pull the tail off the loom, leaving it on the hook. Put to one side.

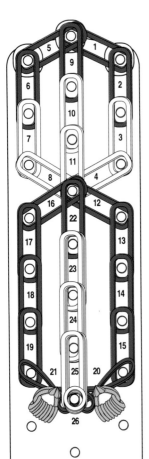

16 Now make the body. With the arrows on the loom pointing toward you, lay out pairs of bands in the colors and order shown, except for bands 23, 24, and 25, which are four bands between each pair of pegs. Bands 20 and 21 are the feet you made in steps 7–10. Add a white cap band to the bottom center peg, twisting it around the peg four times.

17 Place the eyes across the pegs in row 2 and the beak across row 3, and the wings on the outer pegs of row 4. Then place a single black band in a triangle shape over rows 2 and 3, and doubled-over single black bands in a triangle shape over rows 5 and 6.

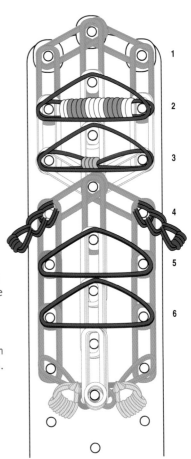

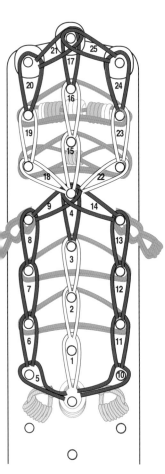

With the help of an adult, use a glue gun or Superglue to glue the penguin to the back of the brooch pin. Allow to cool/dry before wearing.

18 Starting from the bottom center peg, under the cap band and tail, hook the pairs of bands over their opposing pegs in the order shown.

19 Insert your hook into the top peg of the penguin, through all the loops, and gently pull it off the loom. Thread a single black band through all the loops on your hook, thread one end of the band through the other, and pull tight to secure.

20 Attach the tail to the body by inserting your hook into the back of the penguin and pulling one set of the tail loops through to the other side.

21 Then thread one end of the tail loops through the other and pull tight to secure.

22 To complete, thread the remaining loop over the end of the tail to neaten and secure.

fantastic fox

Cunning yet cute, this fox charm will soon be a firm favorite! Using bands in two shades of orange will make your fox look more realistic, but you still get a great effect with just one.

SKILL LEVEL ★★

You Will Need

Loom

58 dark orange bands

20 light orange bands

12 gray bands

12 black bands

32 white bands

Hook

Holding hooks

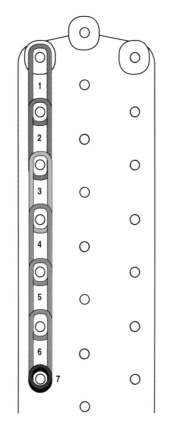

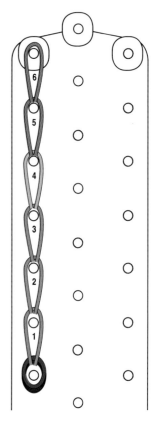

LOOM SETUP

Set up your loom in the diagonal format—3 pegs wide x 13 pegs long (see page 6).

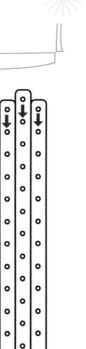

1 Start by making the legs. With the arrows on the loom pointing toward you, lay out doubled-over single bands in the colors and order shown. Add a black cap band to the bottom peg, twisting it around the peg four times.

2 Insert your hook into the bottom peg, under the cap band, and hook the bands over their opposing pegs all the way up the loom in the order shown.

3 Insert your holding hook into the top peg through all the loops and gently pull the leg off the loom, leaving the loops on the hook. Put to one side. Repeat steps 1–3 to make three more legs.

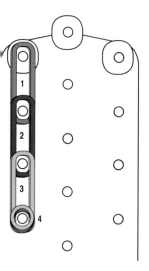

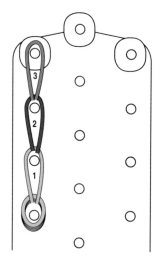

4 Now make the ears. With the arrows on the loom pointing toward you, lay out pairs of bands in the colors and order shown. Add a light orange cap band to the bottom peg, twisting it around the peg four times.

5 Insert your hook into the bottom peg, under the cap band, and hook the bands over their opposing pegs in the order shown.

6 Insert your holding hook into the top peg, through all the loops, and gently pull the ear off the loom, leaving the loops on the hook. Put to one side. Repeat steps 4–6 to make a second ear.

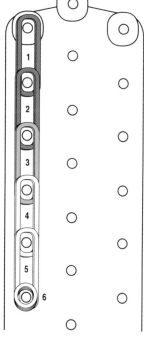

7 Now make the tail. With the arrows on the loom pointing toward you, lay out pairs of bands in the colors and order shown. Add a white cap band to the bottom peg, twisting it around the peg four times.

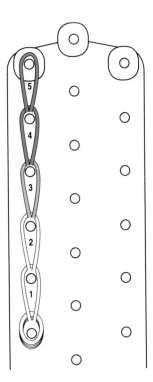

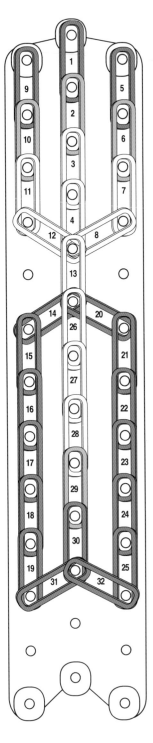

Insert your hook into the bottom peg, under the cap band, and hook the bands over their opposing pegs in the order shown.

Insert your holding hook into the top peg, through all the loops, and gently pull the tail off the loom, leaving the loops on the hook. Put to one side.

10 To make the eyes, wrap a white band around your hook twice, then wrap a black band around it four times, then wrap the first white band around the hook twice more. Repeat with another white and black band to make the second eye.

11 Pull a single white band through all the loops on your hook and put to one side, leaving the loops on the hook.

12 To make the snout, wrap a white band around your hook four times and then pull a single white band through all the loops on the hook, leaving the loops on the hook. Put to one side.

13 To make the nose, repeat step 12 using black bands, this time doubling the band that you thread through the loops on your hook.

14 Pull two white bands through the loops on your hook, leaving the loops on the hook, and put to one side.

15 Now make the body of the fox. With the arrow on the loom pointing toward you, lay out pairs of bands in the colors and order shown.

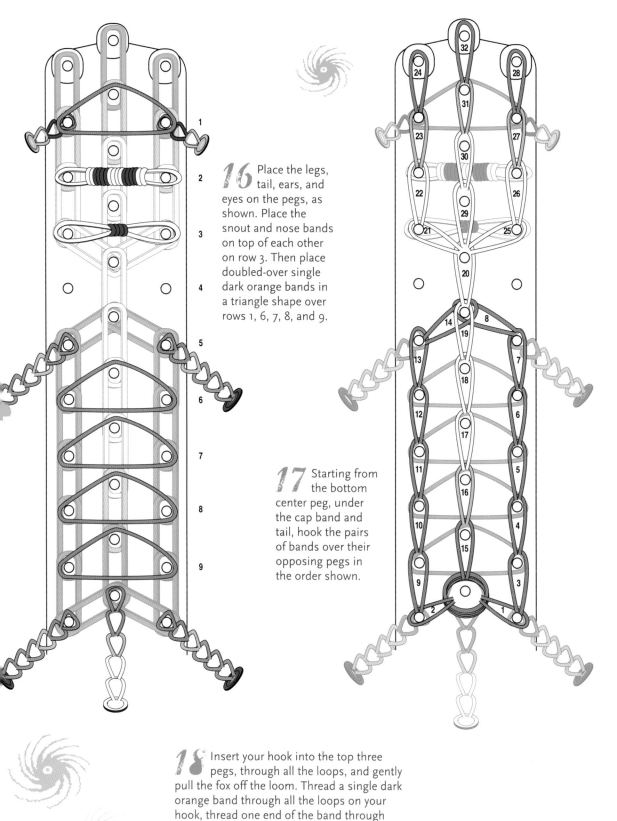

16 Place the legs, tail, ears, and eyes on the pegs, as shown. Place the snout and nose bands on top of each other on row 3. Then place doubled-over single dark orange bands in a triangle shape over rows 1, 6, 7, 8, and 9.

17 Starting from the bottom center peg, under the cap band and tail, hook the pairs of bands over their opposing pegs in the order shown.

18 Insert your hook into the top three pegs, through all the loops, and gently pull the fox off the loom. Thread a single dark orange band through all the loops on your hook, thread one end of the band through the other, and pull tight to secure.

ella the elephant

Make your own little elephant! With her large, flapping ears and cute face, she is sure to cheer up a bag or bunch of keys.

SKILL LEVEL ★ ★

You Will Need

2 looms

249 purple bands

31 pink bands

2 black bands

4 white bands

Hook

Holding hooks

LOOM SETUP

Set up your loom in the V format— 5 pegs wide x 13 pegs long (see page 6). You will need to join two looms together widthwise.

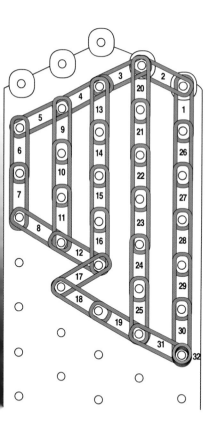

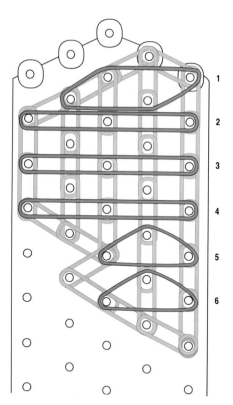

1 First make the ears. With the arrows on the loom pointing toward you, lay out single bands in the colors and order shown. Add a purple cap band to the bottom right peg of the ear, twisting it around the peg four times.

2 Lay out single purple bands horizontally across the rows, except for the band on row 6, which is a doubled-over single band.

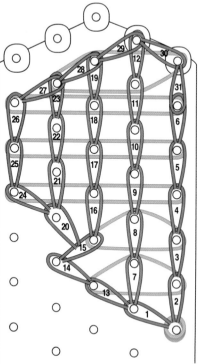

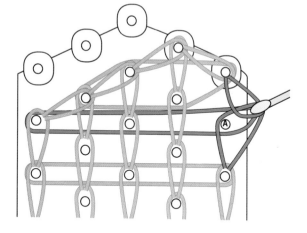

3 Insert your hook into the peg with the cap band, pick up the top band, and hook it over the opposing peg. Repeat all the way up the ear in the order shown.

4 Insert your holding hook into peg A (the last peg that you hooked bands onto), pick up all the loops on the peg, and pull the ear gently off the loom. Put to one side.

5 Repeat steps 1–4 to make a second ear.

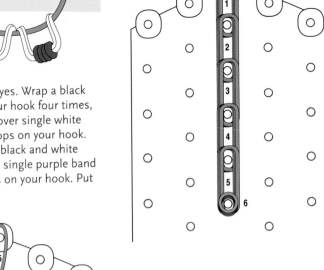

6 Now make the eyes. Wrap a black band around your hook four times, then pull a doubled-over single white band through the loops on your hook. Repeat with another black and white band and then pull a single purple band through all the loops on your hook. Put to one side.

7 Now make the legs. With the arrows on the loom pointing toward you, place three purple bands between pairs of pegs in the order shown. Add a pink cap band to the bottom peg, twisting it around the peg three times.

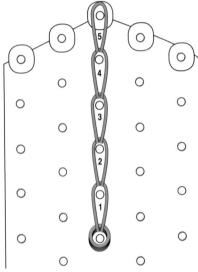

8 Insert your hook into the bottom peg, under the cap band, and hook the bands over their opposing pegs in the order shown.

9 Insert your holding hook into the top band and gently pull the leg off the loom, leaving it on the hook. Put to one side.

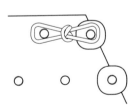

10 Repeat steps 7–9 to make three more legs.

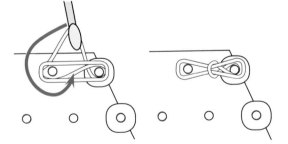

11 To make the tusks, take a single white band and twist once around two pegs in a figure-eight. Then twist it again at one end and place it back over the first peg.

12 Using your hook, pick up the bottom left band and hook it forward over the peg into the center.

13 Repeat step 12 on the right side to complete the tusk. Repeat steps 11–13 to make the second tusk, and put both to one side.

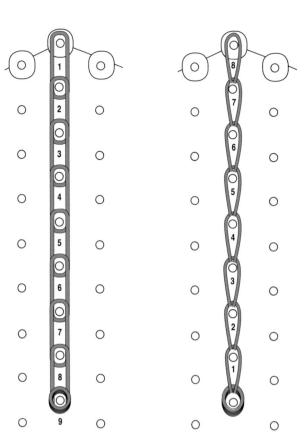

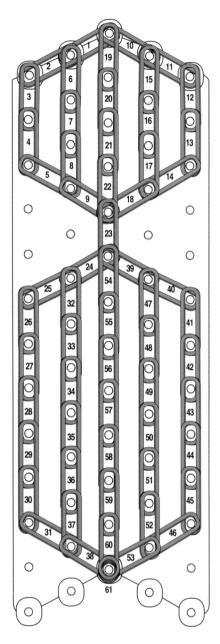

14 Now make the trunk. With the arrows on the loom pointing toward you, lay out doubled-over single purple bands in the order shown. Add a pink cap band to the bottom peg, twisting it around the peg four times.

15 Insert your hook into the bottom peg, under the cap band, pick up the bands, and hook them over the opposing peg. Repeat all the way up the loom.

16 Insert your holding hook into the top peg, through all the loops, and gently pull the trunk off the loom, leaving it on the hook. Put to one side.

17 Now make the head and body. With the arrows on the loom pointing toward you, lay out pairs of purple bands in the order shown. Add a cap band to the bottom center peg, twisting a single purple band around the peg four times.

ella the elephant 83

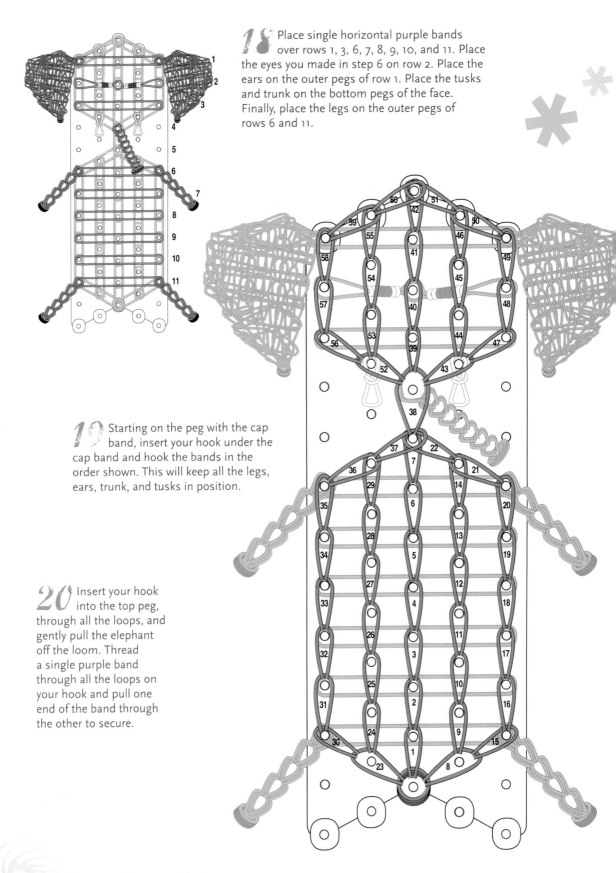

18 Place single horizontal purple bands over rows 1, 3, 6, 7, 8, 9, 10, and 11. Place the eyes you made in step 6 on row 2. Place the ears on the outer pegs of row 1. Place the tusks and trunk on the bottom pegs of the face. Finally, place the legs on the outer pegs of rows 6 and 11.

19 Starting on the peg with the cap band, insert your hook under the cap band and hook the bands in the order shown. This will keep all the legs, ears, trunk, and tusks in position.

20 Insert your hook into the top peg, through all the loops, and gently pull the elephant off the loom. Thread a single purple band through all the loops on your hook and pull one end of the band through the other to secure.

gnasher the alligator

Keep your keys safe with this ferocious alligator keyring!

SKILL LEVEL ★★★

You Will Need

Loom

16 white bands

199 green bands

2 black bands

8 red bands

26 turquoise bands

Hook

Holding hooks

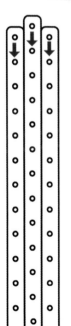

LOOM SETUP

Set up your loom in the diagonal format—3 pegs wide x 13 pegs long (see page 6).

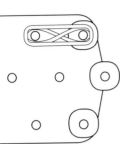
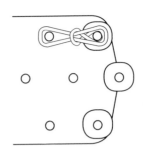
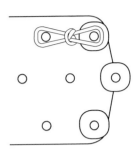

1 First make the teeth. Take a white band and twist it once around two pegs in a figure-eight formation. Then twist it again at one end and stretch it over the same two pegs.

2 Using your hook, pick up the bottom right band.

3 Hook it over the right peg into the center.

4 Repeat step 2 on the left side to make a knot. Take the tooth off the loom and put to one side. Repeat steps 1–4 to make 15 more teeth.

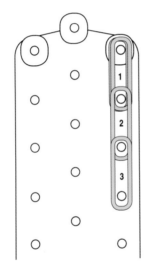

5 Now make the legs. With the arrows on the loom pointing toward you, lay two single green bands over the first pair of pegs, and a doubled-over single green band over each of the next two pairs of pegs.

6 Take a single turquoise band and wrap it around your hook three times.

7 Thread a doubled-over single green band through all the loops on your hook.

8 Thread another doubled-over single green band through the loops on the hook to complete the toe. Repeat steps 6–8 to make two more toes.

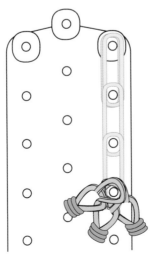
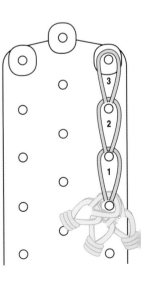

9 Place the toes on the bottom peg of the leg.

10 Insert your hook into the bottom peg of the leg, underneath all the toes, and pull the loops of the doubled-over green band through and onto its opposing peg. Repeat all the way up the leg.

11 Insert your holding hook into the top peg, through all the loops, and pull the leg gently off the loom, leaving it on the hook. Repeat steps 5–11 to make three more legs. Put to one side.

12 Now make the alligator's eyes. Take a black band, wrap it four times around your hook, and thread a doubled-over single red band through all the loops. Repeat with another black and red band, then thread a single green band through all the loops on your hook. Put to one side.

To make your alligator into a keyring, thread a split ring through the loops at the end of the tail.

13 Now make the alligator's upper jaw. With the arrows on the loom pointing toward you, lay out pairs of green bands in the order shown, except for bands 3, 4, 8, and 9, which are single bands, and bands 5 and 10, which are doubled-over single bands. Add a green cap band to the bottom peg, twisting it around the peg four times.

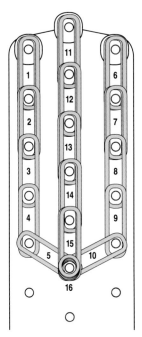

14 Now lay single green bands in a triangle shape over rows 2 and 3, a doubled-over single green band in a triangle shape over row 4, and a doubled-over single band horizontally over row 5.

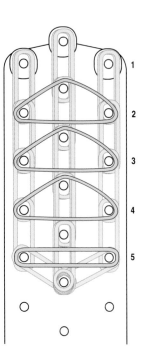

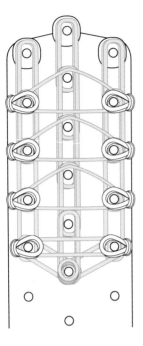

15 Place eight of the teeth made in steps 1–4 on the outer pegs of the jaw, hooking both loops onto the pegs so that just the knot is on the outside edge.

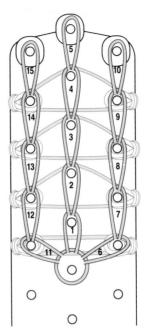

16 Starting from the bottom center peg, insert your hook underneath the cap band and hook the bands in the order shown.

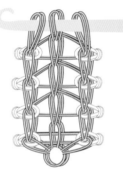

17 Insert your holding hook into the top three pegs, picking up all the loops, and gently pull the upper jaw off the loom, leaving it on the hook. Put to one side.

18 Now make the alligator's lower jaw. With the arrows on the loom facing toward you, lay out pairs of green bands in the order shown, except for bands 6, 7, 10, and 11, which are single bands, and bands 8 and 12, which are doubled-over single bands. For moves 13, 14, and 15, lay out pairs of red bands. Place a green cap band on the bottom center peg, twisting it around the peg four times.

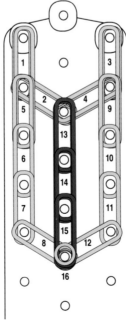

19 Place doubled-over single green bands horizontally over rows 1–4 to hold the mouth together when looped, then place the remaining eight teeth over the outer pegs of the jaw.

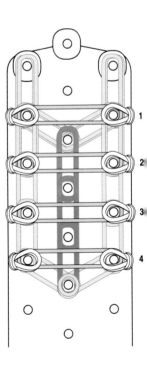

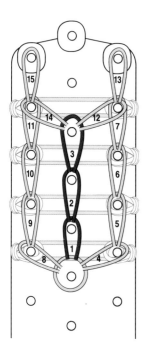

20 Starting from the bottom center peg, insert your hook under the cap band and hook the bands in the order shown. Insert your holding hook into the top three pegs, picking up all the loops, and gently pull the lower jaw off the loom, leaving it on the hook. Put to one side.

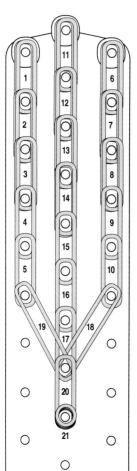

21 Now make the tail. With the arrows on the loom pointing toward you, lay out pairs of green bands in the order shown, except for bands 4, 5, 9, 10, 15, 16, 17, 18, 19, and 20, which are single bands. Add a green cap band to the bottom peg, twisting it around the peg four times.

22 To make the spikes on the alligator's back, wrap a turquoise band around your hook four times and then thread a doubled-over single turquoise band through all the loops. Then take another doubled-over single green band and thread it through all the loops on your hook. Put to one side and make two more.

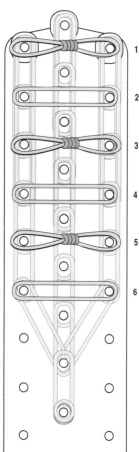

23 Place the spike bands over rows 1, 3, and 5. Place doubled-over single green bands over rows 2, 4, and 6.

24 Starting from the bottom center peg, insert your hook under the cap band and hook the bands in the order shown.

25 Insert your holding hook into the top three pegs, through all the loops, and gently pull the tail off the loom, leaving it on the hook. Put to one side.

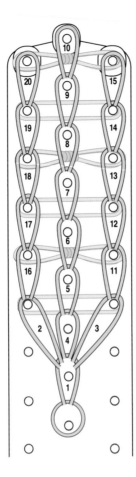

26 Now make the body. With the arrows on the loom pointing toward you, lay out pairs of green bands in the order shown, except for bands 10, 11, 13, and 14, which are single bands, and bands 9, 27, 28, 29, and 30, which are each sets of three bands. Add a green cap band to the bottom center peg, twisting it around the peg four times.

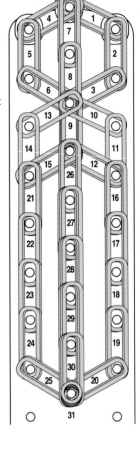

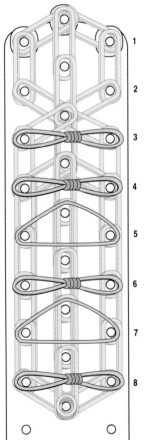

27 Make four more spikes, as in step 22, and place them over rows 3, 4, 6, and 8. Place doubled-over single green bands in a triangle shape over rows 5 and 7.

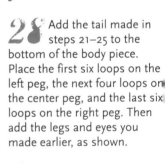

28 Add the tail made in steps 21–25 to the bottom of the body piece. Place the first six loops on the left peg, the next four loops on the center peg, and the last six loops on the right peg. Then add the legs and eyes you made earlier, as shown.

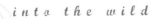

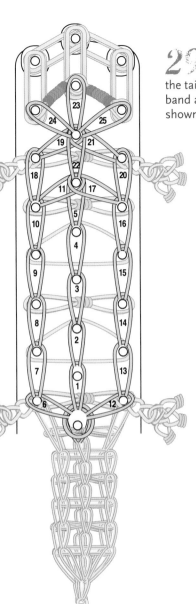

29 Starting from the bottom center peg where you attached the tail, insert your hook under the cap band and begin hooking in the order shown until you get up to the head.

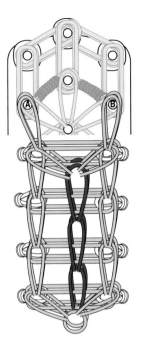

30 Now attach the jaws. Place the four left loops of the lower jaw on peg A and the four right loops on peg B.

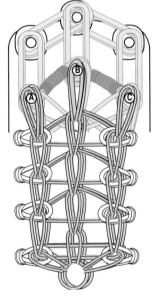

31 Then place the four left loops of the upper jaw on peg A, the center four loops on peg B, and the four right loops on peg C.

32 Hook the remaining bands in the order shown to lock the mouth in place and complete your alligator.

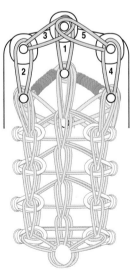

33 Insert your hook into the top center peg through all the loops. Pull the alligator gently off the loom and thread a single green band through all the loops on your hook. Thread one end of the band through the other and pull tight to secure.

olivia the owl

"Twit-twoo!" This owl charm is adorable—why not make it into a necklace? It would be a great Mother's Day gift!

SKILL LEVEL ★

You Will Need

2 looms

58 purple bands

59 turquoise bands

2 dark purple bands

10 yellow bands

12 white bands

Hook

Holding hooks

LOOM SETUP

Set up your loom in the square format—5 pegs wide x 13 pegs long (see page 6). You will need to join two looms together widthwise.

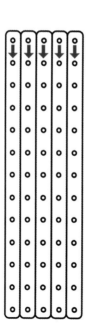

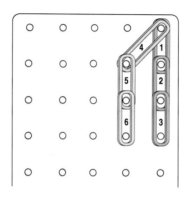

1 First make the owl's wings. With the arrows on the loom pointing toward you, lay out pairs of purple and turquoise bands in the order shown.

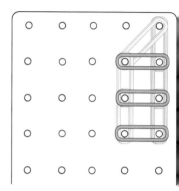

2 Place a doubled-over purple band horizontally over the pegs on rows 2, 3, and 4.

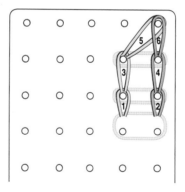

3 Insert your hook onto the bottom left peg and hook the bands in the order shown.

4 Insert your hook into the top peg, pick up all eight loops on that peg, and gently pull them off the loom, leaving it on the hook. Put to one side. Repeat steps 1–4 to make the second wing.

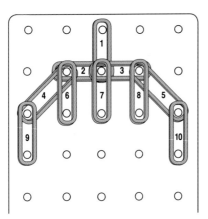

5 With the arrows on the loom pointing toward you, lay out pairs of purple bands in the order shown.

6 Twist a dark purple band four times around your hook and thread two purple bands through the center to create an "eye." Repeat to make the other eye.

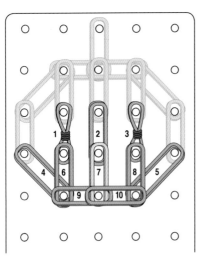

7 Lay the eyes on the loom in the position shown and then continue laying out pairs of purple bands to make the face and a pair of yellow bands to make the beak.

8 Lay out the rest of the owl's body in the order shown, using pairs of turquoise and white bands.

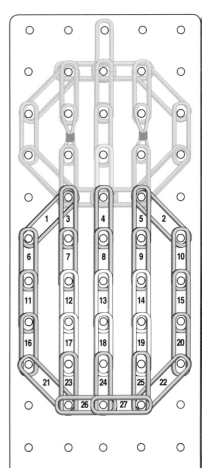

9 To make the feet, twist a yellow band four times around your hook and thread two yellow bands through the center, as in step 6. Repeat to make another foot and place on the loom as shown. Add a cap band in the appropriate color to pegs A, B, and C, twisting them around the pegs four times.

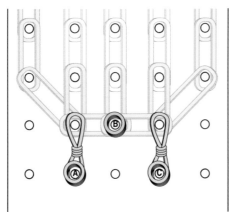

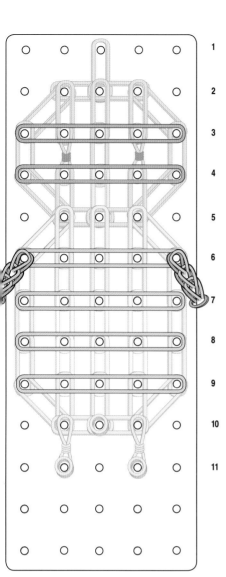

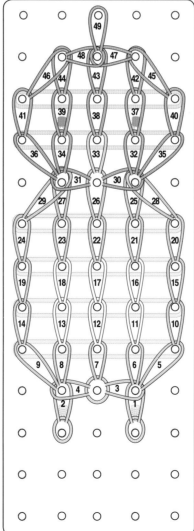

To make the owl into a
necklace, thread it onto
a long silver chain.

10 Place single purple
bands horizontally
over rows 3 and 4. Place
single turquoise bands
horizontally over the pegs
on rows 6 through 9. Finally
add the wings by placing all
the loops of each wing on
the outer pegs of row 6.

11 Starting at the feet,
hook all the bands
over their opposing pegs
in the order shown.

12 Insert your hook
into the top peg
and pull the owl gently off
the loom. Thread one end
of the single loop on your
hook through the center
of the other and pull tight
to secure.

buzzy bees

These bees are so easy and quick to make that you'll have a swarm of them in no time. "Bee" the coolest kid in class by turning them into earrings, too!

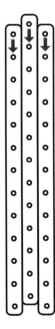

SKILL LEVEL ★

You Will Need

Loom

6 yellow bands

5 black bands

4 blue glitter bands

Hook

LOOM SETUP

Set up your loom in the diagonal format—3 pegs wide x 13 pegs long (see page 6).

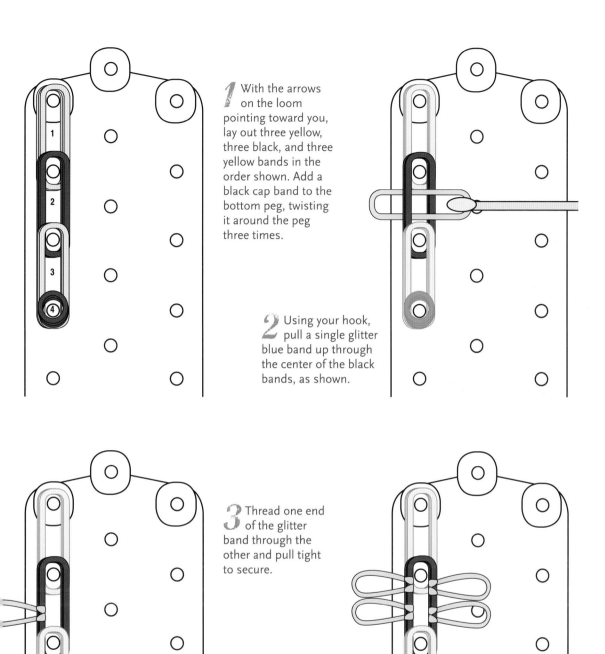

1 With the arrows on the loom pointing toward you, lay out three yellow, three black, and three yellow bands in the order shown. Add a black cap band to the bottom peg, twisting it around the peg three times.

2 Using your hook, pull a single glitter blue band up through the center of the black bands, as shown.

3 Thread one end of the glitter band through the other and pull tight to secure.

4 Repeat steps 2 and 3 once more on the left side of the black band and twice on the right side of the black band.

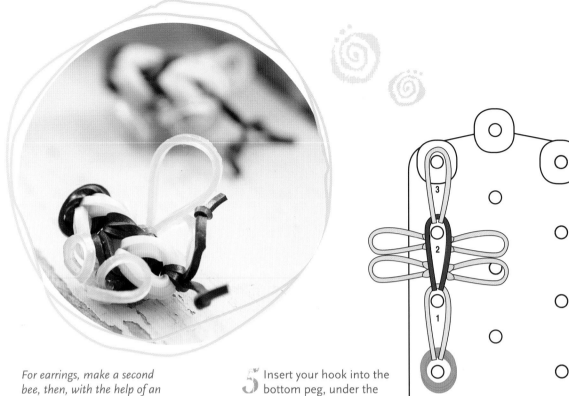

For earrings, make a second bee, then, with the help of an adult, use a glue gun to attach the bee charms onto the backs of clip-on earrings. Allow to cool before wearing.

5 Insert your hook into the bottom peg, under the cap band, and hook the bands over their opposing pegs in the order shown.

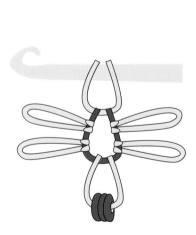

6 Insert your hook into the top peg, through all the loops, and gently pull the bee off the loom, leaving it on the hook.

7 Thread a single black band through all the loops on your hook, thread one end of the band through the other, and pull tight to secure.

8 Cut the black loop in half and tie a knot in each end to create the antennae.

These jelly bands create a really effective dragonfly charm.
Try attaching them to hairclips for a fabulous hair accessory!

flutterby dragonfly

SKILL LEVEL ★

You Will Need

Loom

76 clear bands

20 turquoise bands

28 purple bands

2 black bands

2 yellow bands

Hook

Holding hooks

Glue gun

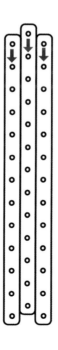

LOOM SETUP

Set up your loom
in the diagonal
format—3 pegs
wide x 13 pegs long
(see page 6).

1 First, make the wings. With the arrows of your loom pointing toward you, lay out doubled-over single clear bands in the order shown. Add a clear cap band to the bottom peg, twisting it around the peg four times.

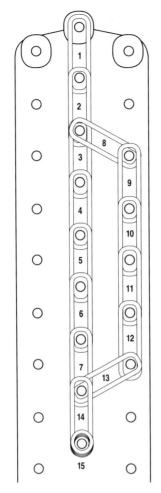

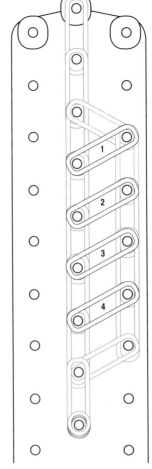

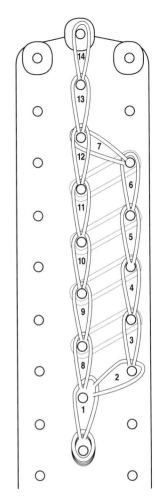

2 Lay doubled-over clear bands diagonally over the pegs, as shown.

3 Insert your hook under the cap band, pick up the bands, and hook over their opposing pegs in the order shown. Continue all the way up the loom in the order shown.

4 Insert your holding hook into the loops on the top peg and gently pull the wing off the loom. Put it to one side, leaving it on the hook. Repeat steps 1–4 to make three more wings.

With the help of an adult, glue the dragonfly charm onto a hairclip using a glue gun or Superglue. Allow to cool before wearing.

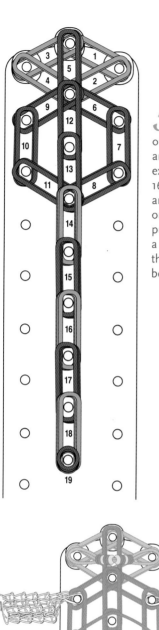

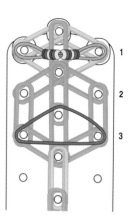

5 Now make the body. Lay out pairs of bands in the colors and order shown, except for bands 14, 15, 16, 17, and 18, which are three bands. Take one turquoise and one purple band and create a cap band by twisting them around the bottom peg four times.

6 Make the eyes by wrapping one black, one yellow, and one purple band around your hook twice. Repeat with another set of bands and then pull a single turquoise band through all the loops on your hook.

7 Place the eyes over the outer pegs of row 1. Then add a single purple horizontal holding band in a triangle shape over row 3, as shown.

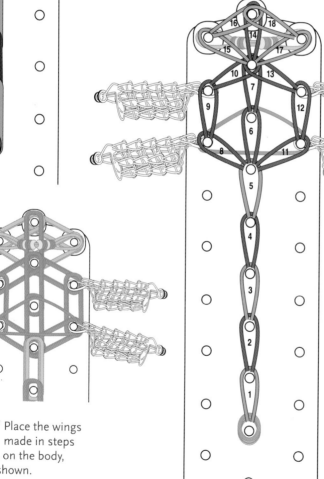

9 Insert your hook into the bottom peg, under the cap band, then pick up the bands and hook them over the opposing peg. Hook the rest of the dragonfly in the order shown.

8 Place the wings made in steps 1–4 on the body, as shown.

10 Insert your hook into the top peg, through all the loops, and gently pull the dragonfly off the loom. Thread a single turquoise band through all the loops, thread one end of the band through the other, and pull tight to secure.

He's the king of the jungle and now he can live on your pencil! His mane looks great with its loopy texture.

leo the lion

SKILL LEVEL ★

You Will Need

Loom

18 yellow bands

55 light orange bands

40 dark orange bands

41 light brown bands

2 dark brown bands

2 white bands

2 black bands

Hook

Holding hooks

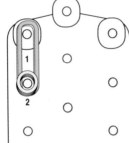
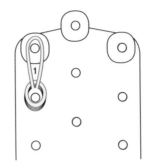

1 First make the ears. With the arrows on the loom pointing toward you, place one yellow and one light orange band between two pegs. Add a yellow cap band to the bottom peg, twisting it around the peg four times.

2 Insert your hook into the bottom peg, pick up the bands under the cap band, and hook them onto the peg above.

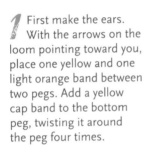

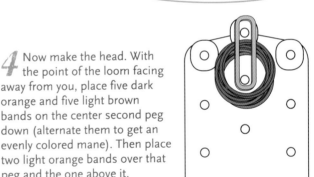

3 Insert your holding hook into the top peg, pick up all the loops, and pull the ear off the loom. Put to one side, leaving the ear on the hook. Repeat steps 1–3 to make a second ear.

4 Now make the head. With the point of the loom facing away from you, place five dark orange and five light brown bands on the center second peg down (alternate them to get an evenly colored mane). Then place two light orange bands over that peg and the one above it.

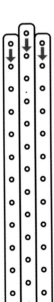

LOOM SETUP

Set up your loom in the diagonal format—3 pegs wide x 13 pegs long (see page 6).

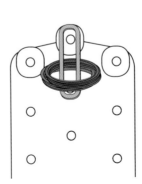

5 Using your hook, pull the loops off the bottom peg and onto the bands between the pegs.

6 Lay out seven more sets of head bands in the same way as in steps 4 and 5, following the colors shown. Bands 8 and 9 are also pairs of bands.

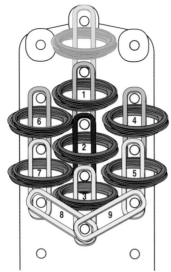

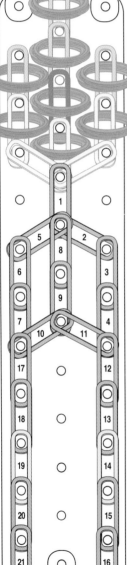

7 To make the body and legs, lay out pairs of bands in the colors and order shown. Add a light orange cap band to the two bottom pegs, twisting them around the pegs four times.

8 Now make the eyes. Wrap a black band around your hook four times, then double up a white band and pull it through the loops on your hook. Repeat with another black and white band and then pull a single light orange band through all the loops on your hook. Put to one side.

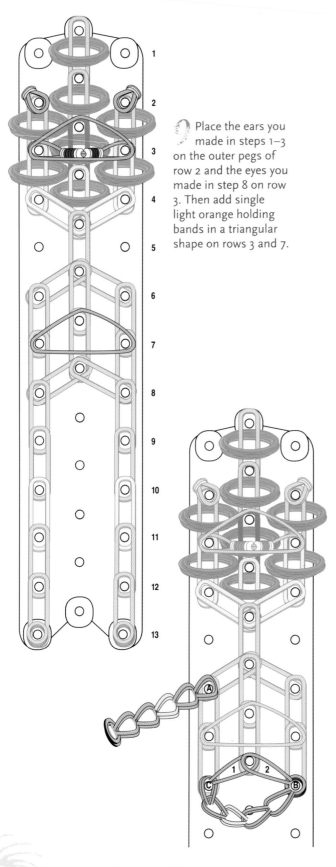

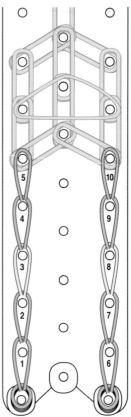

9 Place the ears you made in steps 1–3 on the outer pegs of row 2 and the eyes you made in step 8 on row 3. Then add single light orange holding bands in a triangular shape on rows 3 and 7.

10 Starting from the cap bands on the bottom of the loom, hook the leg bands over their opposing pegs in the order shown.

11 Insert your peg into the top loops of the right leg, pull it off the loom, and place it on the left shoulder peg (peg A). Then pull off all but the top loops of the left leg from the loom and hook the cap band on that leg onto the right hip peg (peg B) so that the leg goes between pegs B and C. Hook the two bottom bands as shown to hold the bottom leg in place.

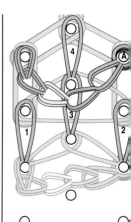

12 Hook the bands on the body over their opposing pegs in the order shown. Then place the cap band of the top leg on the right shoulder (peg A).

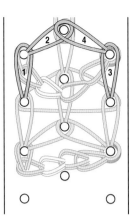

To use the lion as a pencil topper, push a pencil through his legs.

13 Hook the rest of the body bands in the order shown.

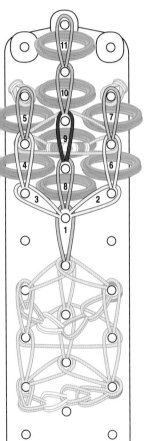

14 Then hook the head bands in the order shown.

15 Insert your hook into all the loops in the top three pegs and pull the lion gently off the loom. Thread a single light orange band through all the loops on your hook, then thread one end of the band through the other and pull to secure.

16 To make the tail, wrap a single light brown band around your hook four times, then pull a single light orange band through all the loops. Thread one end of the orange loop through the other and pull to secure.

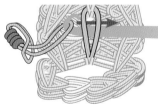

17 Insert your hook into the back of the lion and pull through the tail you made in step 16.

18 Thread the loop that you've just pulled through the lion over the end of the tail and pull tight to secure.

derek the deer

The antlers on this fella are fabulous! Try making a deer or reindeer keyring for your friends and family—it's such a "deer" gift!

SKILL LEVEL ★★

You Will Need

Loom

54 beige bands

6 black bands

2 white bands

56 light orange bands

13 brown bands

102 dark orange bands

Hook

Holding hooks

LOOM SETUP

Set up your loom in the diagonal format—3 pegs wide x 13 pegs long (see page 6).

1 Start by making the antlers. With the arrows of your loom pointing toward you, lay out doubled-over single beige bands between each pair of pegs, as shown. Add a beige cap band to the end of each branch of the antler by twisting a single beige band around each peg four times.

2 Starting from the bottom of the loom, hook the bands over their opposing pegs in the order shown.

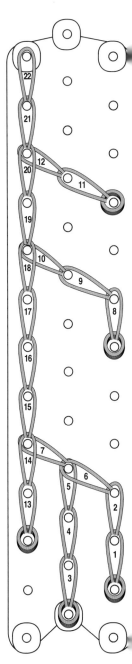

3 Insert your holding hook into the top peg and gently pull the antler off the loom. Put it to one side, leaving it on the hook, and then repeat steps 1–3 to make a second antler.

4 To make the eyes, twist a black band around your hook four times, then pull a doubled-over single white band through the black bands. Repeat this with another white and black band, then pull a single light orange band through all the loops on your hook and put to one side, leaving the eyes on the hook.

5 To make the ears, wrap a brown band around your hook five times, then pull two brown bands through the loops. Put to one side, leaving it on the hook, then repeat to make a second ear.

To make your deer into a keyring, thread a split ring onto either the nose or the tail.

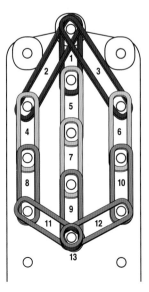

6 Now make the head. Lay out pairs of bands in the colors and order shown. Add a dark orange cap band to the bottom peg, twisting it around the peg four times.

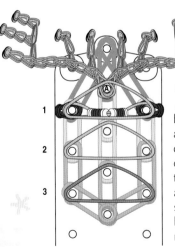

7 Place the ears and then the eyes on row 1, and both of the antlers on peg A, as shown. Then place doubled-over single light orange holding bands in a triangle shape over rows 1 and 2, and a doubled-over single dark orange holding band in a triangle shape over row 3.

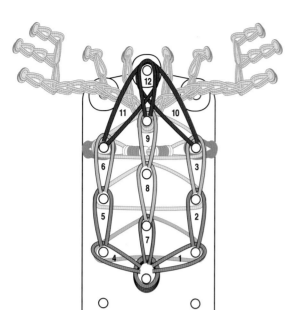

Starting from the bottom of the head, insert your hook into the peg with the cap band, pick up the bottom two bands, and hook them onto the opposing peg. Continue hooking the bands in the order shown.

Insert your holding hook into the top peg and gently pull the head off the loom. Thread a single brown band through all the loops on your hook and thread one end through the other to secure. Wrap a single light orange band around the muzzle to define and shape the head. Put to one side.

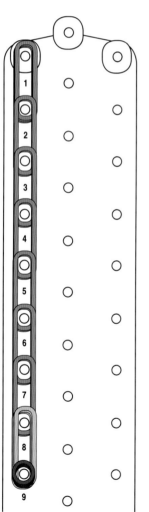

10 Now make the front legs. With the arrows on the loom pointing toward you, lay out pairs of doubled-over single bands in the colors and order shown, except for bands 1 and 8, which are made up of three bands, not doubled. Add a black cap band to the bottom peg, twisting it around the peg four times.

11 Starting from the bottom peg, hook the bands over their opposing pegs in the order shown.

12 Insert your holding hook into the top peg and pull the leg gently off the loom. Put to one side, leaving it on the hook. Repeat steps 10–12 to make a second front leg.

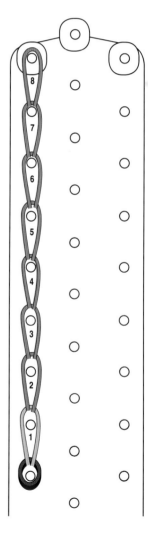

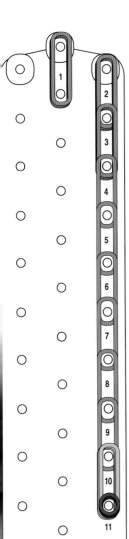

13 Now make the hind legs. With the arrows on the loom pointing toward you, lay out pairs of doubled-over bands in the colors and order shown, except for bands 1, 2, 3, and 10, which are made up of three bands, not doubled. Add a black cap band to the bottom peg, twisting it around the peg four times.

14 Starting from the bottom peg, hook the bands over their opposing pegs in the order shown. Note that band 8 is hooked diagonally onto band 9, not upward.

15 Insert your holding hook into the top two pegs and pull the hind leg gently off the loom. Put to one side, leaving it on the hook. Repeat steps 13–15 to make a second hind leg.

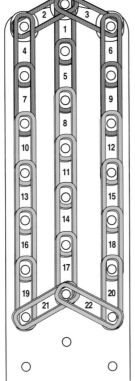

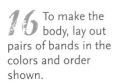

16 To make the body, lay out pairs of bands in the colors and order shown.

17 Following the colors shown, place single holding bands in a triangle shape over rows 2, 3, and 6, and place doubled-over single holding bands on rows 4 and 5. Then add the legs made earlier as shown. Note that the hind legs are spread over two pegs rather than one.

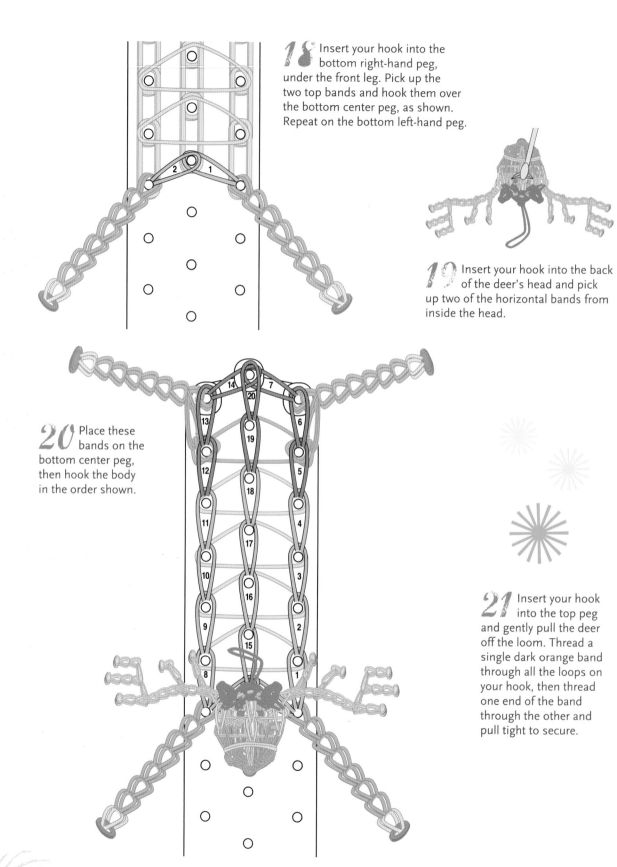

18 Insert your hook into the bottom right-hand peg, under the front leg. Pick up the two top bands and hook them over the bottom center peg, as shown. Repeat on the bottom left-hand peg.

19 Insert your hook into the back of the deer's head and pick up two of the horizontal bands from inside the head.

20 Place these bands on the bottom center peg, then hook the body in the order shown.

21 Insert your hook into the top peg and gently pull the deer off the loom. Thread a single dark orange band through all the loops on your hook, then thread one end of the band through the other and pull tight to secure.

"Pieces of eight!" This cheeky little parrot would look great as a badge on a pirate costume or a winter coat—whichever you prefer!

polly the parrot

SKILL LEVEL ★★

You Will Need

Loom

85 yellow bands

19 orange bands

2 black bands

2 white bands

13 jade green bands

30 blue bands

13 lime green bands

Hook

Holding hooks

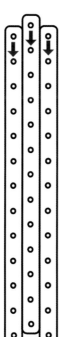

LOOM SETUP

Set up your loom in the diagonal format— 3 pegs wide x 13 pegs long (see page 6).

1 Start by making the beak. Wrap an orange band around your hook four times. Double up two orange bands and pull them through the loops. Then thread a single yellow band through all the loops on your hook. Put to one side.

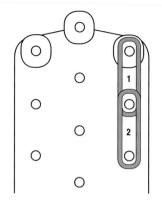

2 Now make the feet. With the arrows of the loom pointing toward you, lay out doubled-over single orange bands as shown.

3 Make the toes by wrapping a single orange band around your hook four times and pulling a doubled-over single orange band through the loops. Make two more of these.

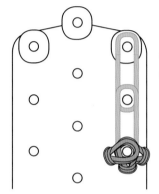

4 Place all three toes on the bottom peg of the foot.

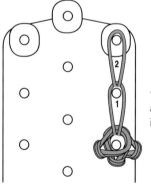

5 Insert your hook under the toes and hook the bands in the order shown.

6 Insert your holding hook into the top peg and pull the foot off the loom. Thread two yellow bands through the loops on your hook and put to one side. Repeat steps 2–6 to make a second foot.

7 To make the eyes, wrap a black band around your hook four times and pull a doubled-over single white band through all the loops on your hook. Repeat with another black and white band. Then pull a single yellow band through all the loops on your hook. Put to one side, leaving the eyes on the hook.

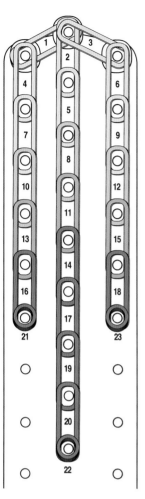

8 Now make the tail. With the arrows on the loom pointing toward you, lay out pairs of bands in the colors and order shown. Add a blue cap band to each of the bottom three pegs, twisting it around the pegs three times.

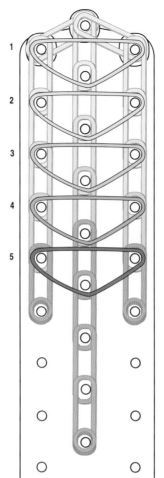

9 Add doubled-over single holding bands in a triangle shape over rows 1–5 in the colors shown.

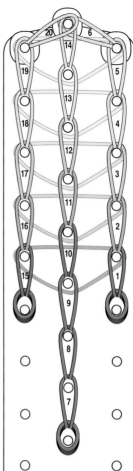

10 Starting from the bottom, hook the bands over their opposing pegs in the order shown.

11 Insert your holding hook into the top peg and gently pull the tail off the loom. Put it to one side, leaving it on the hook.

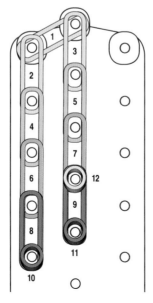

12 Now make the wings. With the arrows of the loom pointing toward you, place single bands (except bands 8 and 9, which are pairs of bands) in the colors and order shown. Bands 10, 11, and 12 are cap bands twisted around the pegs four times.

To make your parrot into a brooch, with the help of an adult, attach a flat-backed badge pin to the back of the parrot using a glue gun or Superglue. Neaten the back by hiding the glue mess with a small square of felt.

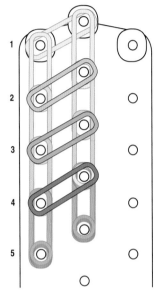

13 Place doubled-over single holding bands diagonally from the left-hand pegs to the pegs in the center on rows 2, 3, and 4, as shown.

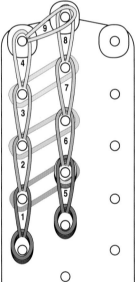

14 Hook the bands over their opposing pegs in the order shown.

15 Insert your holding hook into the top peg and gently pull the wing off the loom. Put to one side, leaving the wing on the hook. Repeat steps 12–15 to make a second wing.

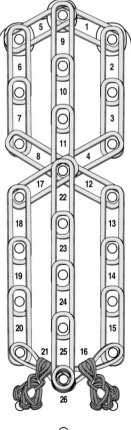

16 Lay out pairs of yellow bands in the order shown to make the body. Note that bands 16 and 21 are the feet made in steps 2–6. Add a yellow cap band to the bottom peg, twisting it around the peg four times.

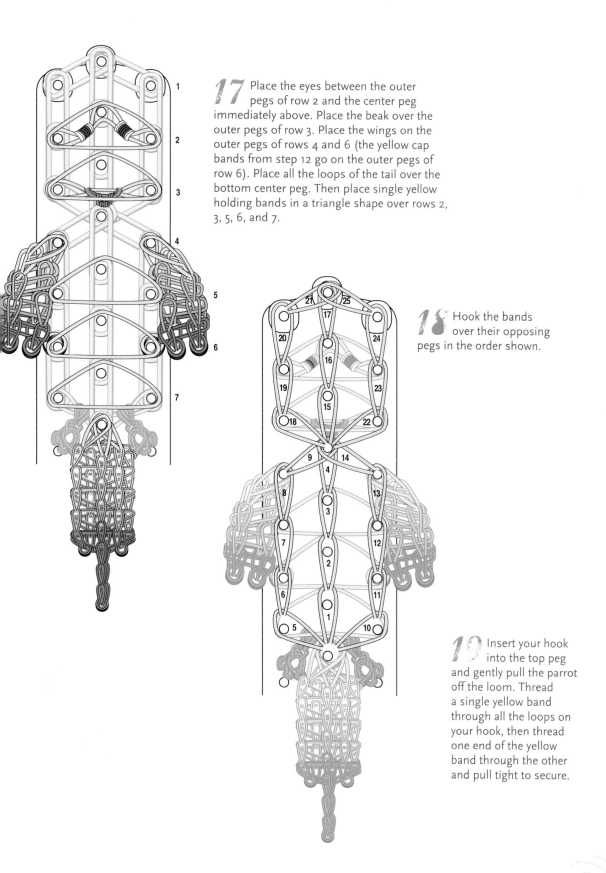

17 Place the eyes between the outer pegs of row 2 and the center peg immediately above. Place the beak over the outer pegs of row 3. Place the wings on the outer pegs of rows 4 and 6 (the yellow cap bands from step 12 go on the outer pegs of row 6). Place all the loops of the tail over the bottom center peg. Then place single yellow holding bands in a triangle shape over rows 2, 3, 5, 6, and 7.

18 Hook the bands over their opposing pegs in the order shown.

19 Insert your hook into the top peg and gently pull the parrot off the loom. Thread a single yellow band through all the loops on your hook, then thread one end of the yellow band through the other and pull tight to secure.

Cheeky monkey! You'll be swinging from the trees once you've mastered this little monkey charm.

funky monkey

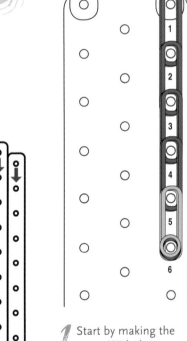

You Will Need

Loom

91 brown bands

32 beige bands

2 black bands

4 white bands

1 red band

Hook

Holding hooks

LOOM SETUP

Set up your loom in the diagonal format—3 pegs wide x 13 pegs long (see page 6).

1 Start by making the arms. With the arrows on the loom pointing toward you, lay out pairs of bands in the colors and order shown. Add a beige cap band to the end peg, twisting it around the peg four times.

2 Starting from the bottom peg, hook the bands over their opposing pegs in the order shown.

3 Insert your holding hook into the top peg and gently pull the arm off the loom. Put to one side, leaving the arm on the hook, then repeat steps 1–3 to make a second arm.

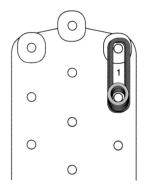

4 To make the ears, place a pair of brown bands between two pegs, with the arrows on the loom pointing toward you, and add two beige cap bands to the bottom peg by twisting them around the peg four times.

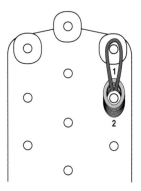

5 Insert your hook into the bottom peg, under the cap bands, and hook the bands onto the top peg.

6 Insert your holding hook into the top peg and gently pull the ear off the loom. Put to one side, leaving it on the hook. Repeat steps 4–6 to make a second ear.

7 To make the eyes, twist a black band around your hook four times, then pull a doubled white band through the black loops. Repeat with another white and black band, then pull a single brown band through all the loops on your hook and put to one side, leaving the eyes on the hook.

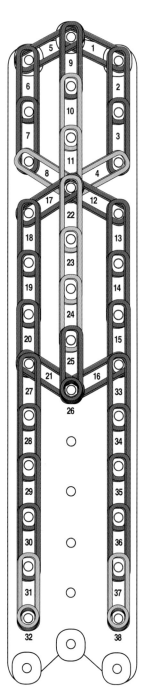

8 Now make the monkey's head, body, and legs. Lay out pairs of bands in the colors and order shown. Bands 26, 32, and 38 are single cap bands, twisted around the pegs four times.

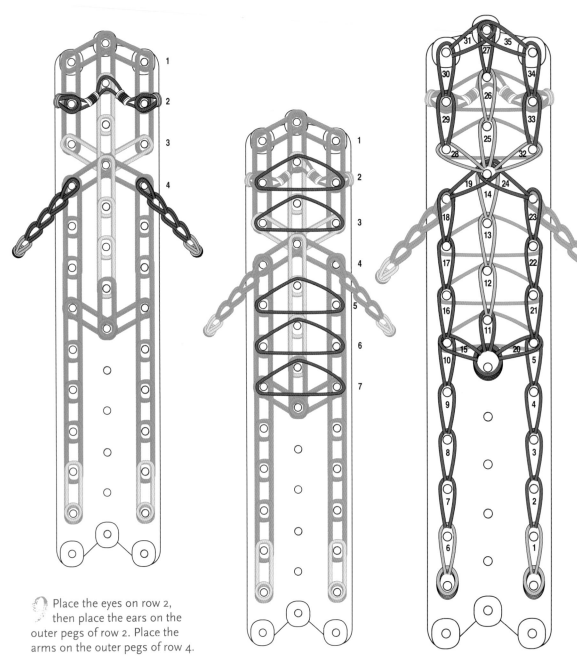

9 Place the eyes on row 2, then place the ears on the outer pegs of row 2. Place the arms on the outer pegs of row 4.

10 Place single brown holding bands in a triangle shape over rows 2, 3, 5, 6, and 7.

11 Starting from the bottom of the right leg, insert your hook into the peg with the cap band, pick up the bottom two bands, and hook them onto the opposing peg. Continue hooking the bands in the order shown.

12 Insert your holding hook into the top peg and pull the body gently off the loom. Thread a single brown band through all the loops on your hook, then thread one end of the brown band through the other and pull tight to secure.

13 Now make the tail. With the arrows on the loom pointing toward you, lay out doubled-over bands in the colors and order shown. Add a beige cap band to the bottom peg, twisting it around the peg four times.

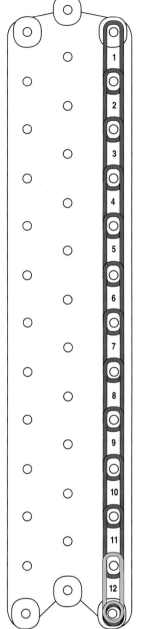

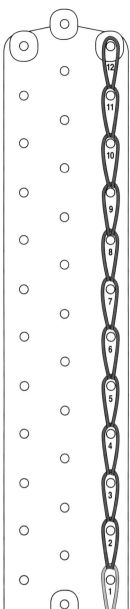

14 Starting from the bottom peg, hook the bands over their opposing pegs in the order shown.

15 Insert your holding hook into the top peg and gently pull the tail off the loom. Put it to one side, leaving it on the hook.

16 To add detail to the face, wrap a single white band around each of the eyes four times to make them pop out, and thread a single red band through the muzzle to make a mouth.

17 To join the tail to the body, thread your hook through the back of the monkey and pull the loops of the tail through. Thread one end of the tail through the tail loops on your hook and pull tight to secure.

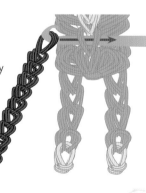

dolly the dolphin

Everyone wants to swim with dolphins!
We can't promise you that, but at least you can make one!

SKILL LEVEL ★★★

You Will Need

Loom

116 blue bands

20 white bands

1 brown band

Hook

Holding hooks

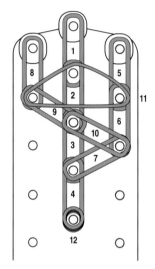

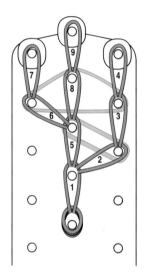

LOOM SETUP

Set up your loom in the diagonal format—3 pegs wide x 13 pegs long (see page 6).

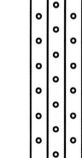

1 Start by making the top fin. With the arrows of the loom pointing toward you, lay out single blue bands in the order shown, except for bands 10 and 11, which are doubled-over singles, and band 12, which is a cap band twisted around the peg four times.

2 Starting at the cap band, hook the bands over their opposing pegs in the order shown.

3 Insert your holding hook into the top three pegs and gently pull the fin off the loom. Put to one side, leaving the fin on the hook.

Make the dolphin into a keyring by threading a split ring through a loop in the top fin.

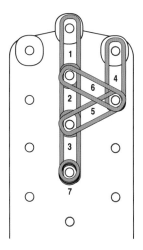

4 Now make the side fins. With the arrows on the loom facing you, lay out single blue bands in the order shown, except for band 6, which is a doubled-over single band, and band 7, which is a cap band twisted around the peg four times.

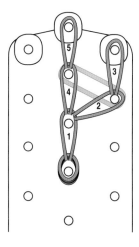

5 Starting from the bottom peg, hook the bands over their opposing pegs in the order shown.

6 Insert your holding hook into the top two pegs and gently pull the fin off the loom. Thread a single blue band through the loops on your hook, then put to one side, leaving the fin on the hook. Repeat steps 4–6 to make a second side fin.

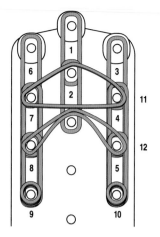

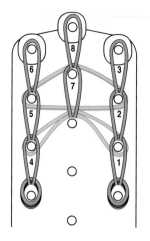

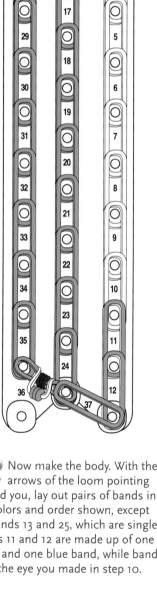

7 To make the tail, lay out single blue bands in the order shown, except for bands 4, 5, 7, 8, and 11, which are pairs, and band 12, which is a doubled-over single. Bands 9 and 10 are cap bands twisted around the pegs four times.

8 Hook the bands over their opposing pegs in the order shown.

9 Insert your holding hook into the top three pegs and gently pull the tail off the loom. Thread two blue bands through the loops on your hook, then put the tail to one side, leaving it on the hook.

10 To make the eye, wrap a blue band around your hook three times, then pull two white bands through the loops on your hook. Leaving this on the hook, wrap a brown band around your hook three times, pull two blue bands through the loops, then pull the brown loops and one end of the set of blue loops through the white loops to complete. Put the eye to one side, leaving it on the hook.

11 To make the nose, wrap a blue band around your hook four times and pull two blue bands through the loops. Put the nose to one side, leaving it on the hook.

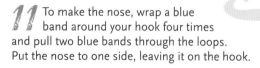

12 Now make the body. With the arrows of the loom pointing toward you, lay out pairs of bands in the colors and order shown, except for bands 13 and 25, which are singles. Bands 11 and 12 are made up of one white and one blue band, while band 36 is the eye you made in step 10.

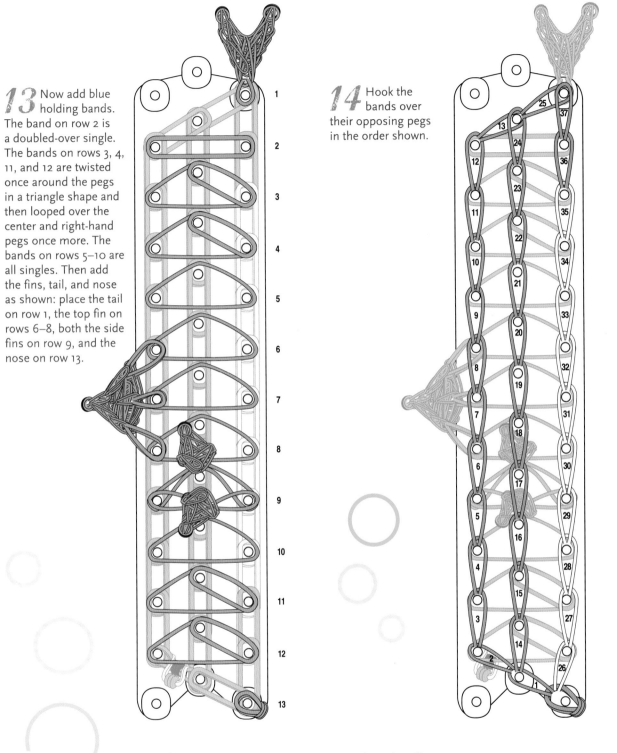

13 Now add blue holding bands. The band on row 2 is a doubled-over single. The bands on rows 3, 4, 11, and 12 are twisted once around the pegs in a triangle shape and then looped over the center and right-hand pegs once more. The bands on rows 5–10 are all singles. Then add the fins, tail, and nose as shown: place the tail on row 1, the top fin on rows 6–8, both the side fins on row 9, and the nose on row 13.

14 Hook the bands over their opposing pegs in the order shown.

15 Insert your hook into the top peg and gently pull the dolphin off the loom. Thread a single blue band through all the loops on your hook, then thread one end of the blue band through the other and pull tight to complete.

ollie the octopus

This fun, eight-legged friend would be great as a keyring or to brighten up a school bag. The method of making this octopus is very different from normal, but it means you only need one loom, not three!

SKILL LEVEL ★ ★ ★

You Will Need

Loom

106 pink jelly bands

4 black bands

32 purple jelly bands

32 turquoise jelly bands

32 lime green bands

8 C-clips

Hook

Holding hooks

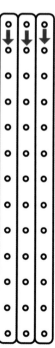

LOOM SETUP

Set up your loom in the square format—3 pegs wide x 13 pegs long (see page 6).

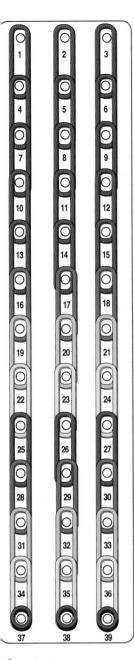

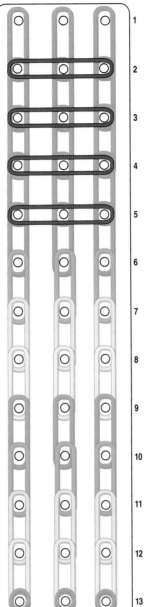

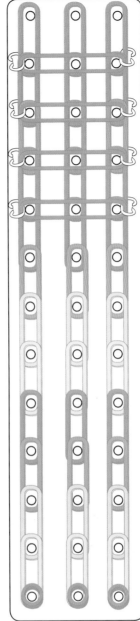

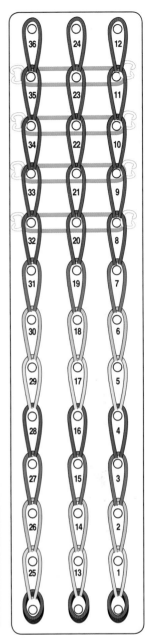

1 With the arrows on the loom pointing toward you, lay out pairs of bands in the colors and order shown. Add pink cap bands to the bottom pegs, twisting them around the pegs four times.

2 Add single pink horizontal holding bands to rows 2, 3, 4, and 5.

3 Add C-clips to the horizontal holding bands. These will help you to pull them across to the other looms later on.

4 Starting from the bottom right, hook the bands over their opposing pegs in the order shown.

5 Insert your holding hook into the top three pegs, through all the loops, and gently pull off the loom. Put these three tentacles to one side, leaving them on the hook.

6 Repeat step 1 but replace the black bands with pink ones.

allie the octopus

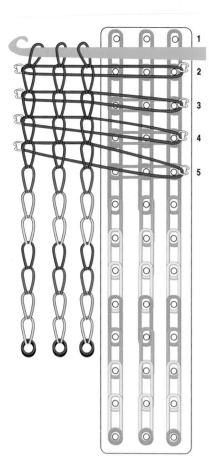

7 Now take the first three tentacles (which are on your holding hook) and pull the C-clips on the right-hand side onto the right-hand pegs of rows 2, 3, 4, and 5. Leave the top three loops on your holding hook.

8 Hook the bands on the loom in the same order as in step 4. Then insert the holding hook with the first three tentacles on it into the top three pegs (you will need to use the wrong end of the hook to do this), and gently pull off the loom. There are now six tentacles of the octopus on your holding hook.

9 Now lay out bands as you did in step 6, but only for two tentacles. Place the left-hand side of the bands that have the C-clips attached over the left-hand pegs of rows 2–5.

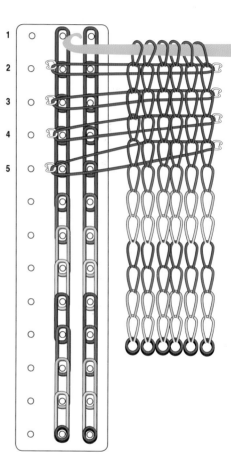

10 Hook the bands in the same order as in step 4.

11 Insert the holding hook through all the loops on the top two pegs and gently pull off the loom.

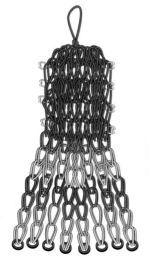

12 Thread a single pink band through all the loops on your hook, then thread one end of the band through the other and pull tight to secure.

13 Remove the C-clips from the octopus as you no longer need them.

To use the octopus as a pencil topper, push a pencil through his legs.

14 Attach another pink band to the single loop by threading it through the loop and then threading one end through the other and pulling tight to secure.

15 Insert your hook into the loops either side of the "seam" in the octopus's body and pull the extended loop through them to secure. Repeat, pulling the same extended loop through each row of loops to "knit" the body together.

Suppliers

The materials you'll need to make the projects in this book are readily available. Some suppliers are listed below.

A. C. Moore (US)
www.acmoore.com

Amazon (US/UK)
www.amazon.com
www.amazon.co.uk

Argos (UK)
www.argos.co.uk

Claire's Accessories (US/UK)
www.claires.com
www.claires.co.uk

Hobbycraft (UK)
www.hobbycraft.co.uk

Hobbylobby (US)
www.hobbylobby.com

John Lewis (UK)
www.johnlewis.com

Michaels (US/Canada)
www.michaels.com

Stuff 4 Crafts (US/Canada)
www.stuff4crafts.com

Tesco (UK)
www.tesco.com

Toys'R'Us (US/UK)
www.toysrus.com
www.toysrus.co.uk

Walmart (US)
www.walmart.com

The Works (UK)
www.theworks.co.uk

Index

Acknowledgments

Thank you to everyone at CICO, especially Carmel and Penny for approaching me to write this latest loopy title! It was great to expand my knowledge of the rubber band techniques I learned when writing *Rubber Band Bracelets*.

Huge thanks must go to the talented illustrator Louise (and her daughter/mini helper, Holly) for their initial Loopy Animal idea after they enjoyed working on the first book so much; to Sarah, the wonderful editor, for all her fabulous ideas and attention to detail; and to Alison, who has done an excellent job of laying out the book. You all worked so hard to get this done in time and I look forward to us working together again in the future.

Final thanks go to my husband, Jamie, for his constant support and help while I was writing this book.